How Your Personality Makes or Breaks Your Child

A SELF-ASSESSMENT GUIDE FOR PARENTS

Dr. Chayanika Singh
Ph.D. Psychology
Specialized in Parent-Child Relationship & Clinical Psychology

UNICORN BOOKS

Publisher
UNICORN BOOKS

F-2/16, Ansari Road, Daryaganj, New Delhi-110002
☎ 011-23275434, 23262683, 23250704 • *Fax:* 011-23257790
E-mail: info@unicornbooks.in • *Website:* www.unicornbooks.in

Branch : Mumbai
23-25, Zaoba Wadi, Thakurdwar, Mumbai-401002
☎ 022-22010941, 022-22053387
E-mail: rapidex@bom5.vsnl.net.in

ISBN 978-81-7806-334-8
How Your Personality Makes or Breaks Your Child

Edition: 2023

Printed at : Param Offsetters, Okhla, New Delhi-110020

REVIEWS

I welcome Dr Singh's contribution to the body of knowledge concerning the roots of disaffection of many of our young, and her determination to ensure that children achieve their optimum potential through the establishment of a positive parenting environment.

David Rowe,
Mentor & Educator (over 20 years of experience with adolescent male delinquents),
Intensive Therapy Unit at Melbourne Juvenile Justice Precinct

The book *How Your Personality Makes or Breaks Your Child—A Self Assessment Guide for Parents* written by Dr Chayanika Singh is worth reading for all would-be or present parents of young children.

It beautifully depicts, how small 'care' or 'negligence' (knowingly or unknowingly) can make or break a child's personality. Children are the future parents. Any deviation of their normal mental growth can become a vicious circle and it may not only affect the concerned family, but the entire society, in due course of time. Not only the working parents, the non-working mothers should also take 'small cares' to understand their children and help in their overall development.

I shall recommend this book to all the parents and grandparents to know and make a bond with our upcoming generation. Kudos to Dr Chayanika Singh for this illustrative book on a vital topic.

Dr Krishna Kumar Mallick
Faculty of Medicine, AIMST University, Malaysia

Every parent loves to have children but many of them fail to manage them. This book, by Dr Chayanika Singh, is a complete handbook on disciplining children and parents. Everybody should read it to create a decent family and society.

Dr K. N. Jehangir
Former Director, ICSSR, New Delhi

The book, *How Your Personality Makes or Breaks Your Child: A Self-Assessment Guide for Parents,* is an attempt to help the readers to manage their own as well as their children/adolescents' concerns. The book is an attempt to make the field of psychology not only interesting and understanding but also practical, rejuvenating, and most importantly, as scoring as any sub-field of psychology. This book shows the parents the real world of children and adolescents through its blend of cutting-edge of practical applications. I am sure this volume will be very useful as a guide to handle self, and others in the world of high competitive demands.

Prof. Dr N. K. Chadha,
Professor and Head, Department of Psychology
Former Head and Director,
Department of Adult Continuing Education and Extension
Former Chairman, Board of Research in Social Science and Humanities

Many of the parents are not aware that their personality traits and parenting styles have a profound impact on their children. They, therefore, need to realise that the parent-child relationships consist of a combination of behaviours, feelings, and expectations that are unique to a particular parent and a particular child. This book makes them realise how their own weaknesses like anxiety, anger, hostility, depression, rigidity, etc. are coming on the way of healthy personality development of their children. It also says further how love, affection, care, and encouragement make their children well-adjusted and emotionally balanced. Apart from these factors, impact of some other factors like reward and punishment, rejection and neglect has also been examined by the author in detail. This book is thus an eye-opener, thought-provoking, and worth reading by each one of us, particularly parents.

Dr M. B. Sharan (Ex Prof. IIT Kharagpur)
Senior Professor of Psychology,
School of Humanities & Social Sciences,
Indian Institute of Technology, Patna, Bihar

Much needed book in the crises as a good parenting guide & advice. An excellent gift for the parents & would be parents in the form of a conversational book.

Dr (Mrs) Shefalika Verma
Sahitya Akademi Awardee, 2012
President: Women & Child Development under International Maithili Council, Ranchi

Excellent book on preventive mental health issues of a child & adolescent through good parenting. This book promotes positive family mental health leading to societal well being. It's a real use of best & positive side of psychology.

It is highly recommended for parents, future parents so that they are able to grow and develop psychologically healthy and responsible citizens of the world.

Prof. (Dr) Abha Singh
Director, Amity Institute of Psychology & Allied Sciences

A child is never too young to learn. He starts absorbing from his environment and emulating his parents before they are ready for it. This book is a reality check of sorts that asks parents to look within themselves before accusing, blaming, scolding or bossing over a child. All the more most parents are oblivious to the mistakes they make.

How Your Personality Makes or Breaks Your Child: A Self-Assessment Guide for Parents is a storehouse of practical tips to live happily ever after. Not only is it a road map to help a child blossom into a good human being, but it is a guide to help a parent be the person they want their child to be.

Mrs Brinda Sarkar
The Telegraph

This book is an encyclopedia of parenting—timely & precisely written. It serves the parents & parenting-solutions in a practical manner. A must read.

Prabhat Khabar

Acknowledgement

I convey my gratitude to Dr Sujata Ghosh, Dr S.K. Somani, Dr S.K. Khanna, Dr Taparia, Dr B.K. Binani, Dr B.P. Shah, Dr Drishti Kothari, Dr Ruma Ray, Dr A.K. Jain, Dr Rupa Sharan Ganguli, Dr Gulgulia, Dr Sarbani Khanna, Mr Dayanand Gupta and to my husband, Dr Hridaya Narayan Singh, who gave me numerous opportunities to analyse family dynamics and different relationships among family members by referring a number of families to me for counselling to solve conflicts arising from their interpersonal relationships.

My thanks go to Mr Martyn Brown, Ms. Seema Mohta, Mr Moloy Banerjee, Ms. Pushpa Tiwari, Mr Anurag Kedia, Aditya, Anshuman and Amrita for their direct and indirect involvements in the development of the book.

I am grateful of Mr Suranjan Roy and Mrs Nina Mehra for helping me proofreading this book. A very special thanks to my son, Chanakya Hridaya, for being my biggest critic and my biggest supporter and to my daughter, Neha Hridaya , who has always had immense faith in me and was a constant source of motivation while writing this book.

Special thanks to Ms. Brinda Sarkar of the Telegraph, Mr Ajay Vidyarthi (Prabhat Khabar), Mr Sanjay Binani, who often guided me in giving a proper shape to the original manuscript into a book.

Finally, I'm thankful to Ms. Madhu Neotia & Shree Govindramji Agarwal, Shree Rajendrji Kedia, who selected me to be the part of their hospitals, Bhagirathi Neotia, Women & Child Care Centre & Marwari Relief Society Hospital respectively & the doctors, staff and members of the same hospitals who have given me immense opportunities to deal with the cases related to Parent-Child Relationship.

Preface

Expression is the foundation of a loving and stable relationship. This book is for those parents who love their children heart and soul but lack the quality of expression. Your innocence or ignorance may turn your child, with an innocent mind into a difficult child. The objective behind writing this book is not to instil fear in parents or would-be parents. While going through this book, they can outline their issues and assert themselves in the right direction. Every parent has certain flaws and that is normal. This book aims at giving everyone an opportunity to introspect, without any dispute, because everyone has unique problems and those are to be managed accordingly. This book serves as a mirror through which you can view yourself truly and clearly. Sometimes, we, as parents, make lots of mistakes in the way we rear our children, and some of these mistakes are unavoidable. But being parents, we need to identify the repercussions of our own problems on our kids, and look for options to mitigate any adverse impact on them.

Don't shed tears at your child's misdeeds. Have an analytical outlook and set aside any guilt feeling you might be harbouring against yourselves; instead, enjoy your precious moments with your child. Be transparent with your identity and sort out your issues successfully.

Come closer to yourself

- Your own problems hinder your child's progress
- Mental disturbances between spouses, resulting in the parents quarrelling at home inter se, are a great mental trauma for a child.
- Know yourself through your child's eyes
- Train yourself as a good parent
- Be your child's best friend, guide and philosopher. Protect yourself from old-age worries

- Your child's bright future is your old-age asset
- This book is full of tips on how to manage yourself and the best ways to handle your young child and adolescent as well.

Have you ever felt that sometimes you have to be cruel to be kind? Have you ever drawn a dividing line between too much and too little? Is it not a good thing to perceive yourself honestly and adequately in case you are missing out on your own issues? Come on! Do not try to shy away from your own prejudices; nor do you ever think of keeping yourself at arm's length from your deviating child on account of your own egocentricity, vanity or susceptibility. Accept them and deal with them accordingly. After all, it is a matter of your child's psychological welfare. What is wrong if you find the solutions by assessing yourself? Give it a try!

Violating social norms is a crime. Crime, in any form—including drug addiction and alcoholism—hangs like the sword of Damocles over our heads, ruining many families. Our own blood kills us, either physically or psychologically. Aren't we parents responsible for these heinous happenings? If we want to stop this, the very first step to stop crime is to make ourselves aware of our children's behavioural pattern and assess them scrupulously.

My objective behind writing this book is not to correct children who have become delinquent, but to understand children unbiasedly and prevent them from turning into criminals. Criminality is not a sudden step or reaction to a child's unhealthy environment or bad parenting, but is a slow negative development, which leads them to take the most dreadful and ultimate step. My aim in writing this book runs in the direction of disciplining parents for winning the battle of children who are prone to misconduct, who might go astray eventually. I believe that good parenting is the solution to any type of child centric problems—be it big or small.

Criminality or addiction is not a disease. It's an accumulation of turbulent feelings or emotions, a negative behavioural syndrome that begins to develop in a child just when parents find themselves incapable of managing him or her fully. Every criminal has a family. So the problems in the family and the characteristics of the parents have a long-lasting effect on the child's behavioural pattern.

Several reasons exert influence over your child's behaviour either positively or negatively, like—

— Genetic factor

— Parents' own personality and temperament

— Parents' state of socialization

— Marital discord

— Parenting style

— Child's own temperament

This book sheds light on the problems and issues of parents. Even genetic problems can be managed by a good parenting style.

Alcohol, drugs, gambling, betting, and substance abuse are major problems which our children will face while growing up. Lack of remorse and conscience in a child acts as a signal for all of us to be alert, because our children may have difficult temperament which need careful and delicate parenting. Suicide is also an indirect/passive mode of crime which is knowingly/unknowingly committed by our children due to lack of proper supervision and awareness of the parents.

Instances of suicide and delinquency in children are becoming frequent and alarming. Blaming only academic pressure is wrong. Children are born with several academic and non-academic talents; if we provide them a peaceful ambience and loving approach, the children can perform excellently. Trust them.

In my long years of experience in dealing with children affected by psychological problems, I have found that most behavioural issues in children can be traced back to their parents' own personalities, their strengths and weaknesses. The increased incidence of conduct-disorder in children (which often develops into criminality, alcoholism or drug-addiction and suicidal tendencies in adulthood) is a cause for grave concern amongst parents the world over.

Considering that the parents' own problems form the essential basis for the child's behavioural pattern, I invariably inquire into parents' problems before delving into their children's issues. Through this book,

I hope to assist parents in exercising discipline, which poses both a challenge and an opportunity. Good parenting, the features of which I have outlined in the book, will, I believe, eventually help parents create bonds of love for, and trust in, their children, which, in turn, will go a long way towards prevention of their children from developing psychological problems assuming dimensions later on.

For convenience of writing, I have used 'he' to represent both boy or girl for the children, in this book.

I hope this book will serve as a 'beacon light' for every parent and would-be parent.

Dr Chayanika Singh

chayanika.singh8@gmail.com
Ph: (0) 9831309411

Recommendation

It gives me an immense pleasure in writing that Dr Chayanika Singh, one of my students, has taken pain to author a book entitled, *How Your Personality Makes or Breaks Your Child*. This book is a unique mirror through which parents can judge themselves whether they are doing justice to their children or not. If not, they are advised to take corrective actions. The author deserves praise for providing guidelines for parents or would-be parents in successfully managing their children's behavioural pattern. Among others, she has, in general, hinted towards three basic *mantras* for healthy development of a parent-child relationship.

(a) Parents should provide emotional support to their children by understanding their issues and by involving themselves into their children's lives

(b) Parents should exercise proper control over their behavioural pattern by encouraging matured behaviour among their children

(c) For promoting self-reliance among children, parents should provide autonomy to them.

Sometimes, the problems may be with the parents. Still, they can be a good guide to their children by adopting to a good parenting style characterised by being attentive, patient, and sensitive to their needs. Throughout the book the author has laid emphasis on good parenting which tends to create bonds of love and affection with, and trust in, their children, and has further proved to be experimentally and empirically a healthy practice and guide.

The key suggestion given in the book for the parents and would-be-parents is to adopt a good parenting style, popularly known as authoritative style (far distinct from authoritarian style), while bringing up their children. This style is clearly associated with many aspects of competence such as self-control, task persistence, upbeat mood and cooperation during preschool years; and at advance ages, high self-esteem, and responsiveness to parents' views, appreciable school performance as well as social and moral maturity among children.

Once again, I thank Chayanika for providing a beacon of light for guiding all those parents who would be taking advantage of this book in discharging their onerous responsibilities, vested in them as parents, lest their marriage would go on the rocks, and ruination of their children's lives may take place.

Arun Kumar Singh
University Professor & Former Head Deptt. of Psychology
Patna University

Dedication

A good childhood is the strength
of my life.

Ma, Papa — Pranam

CONTENTS

Reading This Book
Is Learning Yourself

INTRODUCTION

I still have some vivid memories of my childhood and I can't but reminisce. I had a close-knit group of friends and we spent our leisure time frolicking and playing with each other. Those blissful summer (and winter) days were the happiest of our lives and seemed as if they would last forever. However, not everything was as perfect as they seemed to be. I was always left with lingering doubts in my mind. I would often ask myself: "Are all of us happy?" "Is everybody's life truly perfect?" And even at that early age, the answer to those questions seemed crystal clear: NO.

I remember one of my friends, Kaka, who was very decent and well-behaved. We used to tease him because of his timidity and his straightforwardness. One day, as we were sitting together in a playground, I observed him killing ants which were moving in a straight line on their way to their nest. I cried out, "Kaka! Why are you killing these helpless creatures?"

He replied promptly and with a touch of bitterness, "I despise it when they go in such a disciplined way." I was left speechless as he continued eliminating the ants one by one.

Another incident concerning Kaka immediately springs to my mind. It was late in the evening and we were still playing, being oblivious of the time. Suddenly, Kaka's mother appeared on the scene, and before we could realise what was happening, we heard a loud smack. Two terrible slaps were blown on Kaka's cheeks. We were terrified into silence, but Kaka, with his cheeks crimson due to the blows, said not a word and shed not a drop of tear. The very insult that the slaps carried must have been a thousand times worse than the pain they inflicted, but he went on his way home with his mother, quietly as ever. For days afterwards, he refused to talk to anybody in the class. I could not help feeling sorry for him. But more than that, I felt a tremendous anger against his parents, who, I was sure, with their actions, would turn such a wonderful boy into a shadow of his usual self.

I was forced to say to myself:

"How can a mother teach her son to be disciplined being so indisciplined herself?"

As the years went by, Kaka became increasingly irritable and withdrew into his shell. He had become totally non-communicative and his parents finally resorted to sending him to a boarding school, thinking that this would be the solution to all their problems. When he came home during the vacations, he seemed quite happy. He then revealed to me one of his secrets and that's when I discovered how much he had changed from the sweet and simple boy all of us used to adore.

I will never forget what he told me. "I have just learnt how to make a bomb. It's simple. Just take a fused bulb, make a little hole in it and fill it up with some explosive, the kind used in firecrackers. Keep it in a remote place and throw a burning paper on it. It's the greatest feeling in the world when it explodes and you feel a rush of adrenalin through your veins." I had nothing to say. I was left numb inside and felt helpless as I thought of what Kaka had turned into. I realised that I had lost my friend forever.

I needed to share my thoughts with someone and so I turned to my best friend, Simran. I told her every word of what Kaka had said to me and I made my anger directed at his parents very apparently. I asked her how someone could have parents so uncaring and who, with their severity, had turned Kaka into that monster. Much to my surprise, it was Simran who broke down crying, inconsolably. The tears drowning out every word she attempted to say. Simran and Kaka had never been close to each other hence, I could not understand the reason for her outburst. When she settled down, I asked her what had happened. She was initially hesitant in revealing her reasons, but I managed to coax it out of her through calm and endearing words. Simran told me how her parents were going through a rough phase. They would shout and argue all the time and it seemed as if they had lost their mutual love for each other. Things had reached such a sorrowful pass that she felt like an alien in her own house and hated returning home, and, at the same time, apprehending they would treat her as a mediator between the two. The way she sobbed between words, moved me so much that I decided to pen the incident in my diary with the title:

Why do these sweet kids have such cruel parents?

I returned home and reflected and introspected for long about these couple of incidents. I realised that if I had so little idea of what my closest friends were going through, I could not even imagine what the other children in school were being subjected to at home. Kaka's parents might have worked hard to make him a good kid. But why were the desired results reversed?

My life has continued to revolve around these incidents. That very day, I made a promise to myself: I would not let any other child suffer the way my friends had suffered. When I completed high school I made up my mind to take up psychology as a subject so that I would be able to understand the root cause of the problems faced by the children and how their parents unwittingly help in the development of behavioural and psychological disorders. With this book, I hope, I have succeeded in getting a little closer to achieving the goal, I set out to achieve.

In the years that I have spent in my clinic in Calcutta, I have experienced many interesting cases and they have given me the reflection of my childhood experiences. Needless to say, they have kept me inquisitive. The more I started handling these cases, the more they started growing on my psyche and slowly I got involved in them. The memories of my childhood continued to be the driving force behind my quest to strike at the root of parent-child conflicts. Whenever I dealt with a parent-child relationship, every time I have felt that Kaka was murmuring in my ears...

"Why so late?...Why was there none of my parents?"

The distressed look of Kaka has been chasing me and compelling me to delve further into the problems of the parent-child relationship. I decided to go on a journey to discover the essential basis of differences arising within a family by assessing the cases related to parent-child issues.

Children, from their infancy, are a replica of clay on a potter's wheel. Just as a potter creates beautiful objects of art on his wheel, parents play the role of moulding and influencing their children to develop into complete human beings in their life. Is it not our duty to help our children develop into good human beings? In the course of my life, I have seen many Kakas around me, with a steady dose of undesirable aggression injected into them and bustling with restless energy, ever engaged in making various devices for destruction. My range of vision and understanding started from that point. Those Kakas still haunt me. There are ample cases, which motivated me to help children like Simran and Kaka. It was in the light of these encounters that I came to the inevitable conclusion that moulding a child in the right manner is the primary responsibility of parents.

It is perhaps a suitably reliable generalisation that no parent would ever willingly try to harm their child or pursue any course of action which would adversely affect the child. However, it is also true that parenting, far from being an inherited quality, is an acquired skill. It is an art, which, as is the case with any other talent, in order to be perfected, has to be wrought upon, on the slow grind of self-realisation and empathetic perception.

As I handled more of such cases related to children, in pursuance of my profession, I was stunned to detect the marked effect of the inherent characters of the parents on the upbringing of their child. However, the parents seemed unable or unwilling to visualise that their questionable behaviour was creating an adverse impact on their child. I realised that parents were 'innocent culprits' because they were unintentionally sowing the seeds of negative traits in the 'innocent mind' of their offspring. No sensible parent would wish to push their child into the realms of darkness. But the pity was that, the parents declined to become aware of their own negative behaviour, which was becoming detrimental to the progress of their child and could lead to dire consequences in future.

Parents should be rational about their behaviour. A child apes their negative behaviour quickly. It is easier to imbibe negative traits than positive ones. Parental aggression, either latent or manifested, ends up in promoting more aggression or hostility in their child, and, as a result, they may develop, nourish and maintain the tendency to overpower parents' negative treatment through counter-aggression whenever they avail of the latitude to generate their own ideas for their behaviour and action.

I have also observed that, parents, unfortunately, fail to identify the positive traits of their kids. Instead, they engage themselves in making the futile and fatal mistake of highlighting their children's faults, mistakes and misdeeds. Consequently, they miss out the opportunity to appreciate them and end up in distancing themselves from their child. This gap can only be bridged through a profound understanding of not only their child's troubles but also their own problems which, ultimately, assume dimensions.

There is a strong link between parents' own inner psyche and its manifestation in their outward behaviour. How parents behave with their child is a definite reflection of how they view themselves in the mirror of their child's eyes. It is of fundamental importance to note that the parents' own problems are woven into their child's problems and this interlocking mesh can only be unravelled when they perceive the threats posed by both these sets of uncertainties. Parents, unaware of this conundrum, are unable to see their child's faults in the light of their own behaviour, and thus forcefully try to fix a problem which stems from their own troubles. This is a sad state of affair and a startling revelation of truth, too. No good can come out of replacing the stem of a plant, whose origin actually lies in the roots, hidden deep beneath the soil. It is only when parents become conscientious that they can truly understand the trials and tribulations faced by their own child, who, metaphorically and literally, turns out to be the faithful reflection of their parents. It is time for parents to wake up and look at this new reality and come to terms with their own selves before they blame their children for their mistakes.

As I started analysing the real causes of parental problems, surprisingly, my antagonism towards Kaka's parents started subsiding. In the light of my new-found realisations, I saw that Kaka's parents might have had their own personal troubles, which, in the manifestation of their superficial behaviour, had unwittingly caused the transformation of Kaka from a sweet, innocent child, he used to be, into an unfortunate offender he had become. I was shocked to know parents' naivety while tackling the small problems of their child. Their ignorance of how their own behaviour influences or anticipates the behaviour-pattern of their kids, was an eye-opener for me. Parents are not aware that their problems are perceived by their child from the very age, when they start taking their incipient steps. Problem arises from the unconsciousness that the children are too young to understand. The learning and imbibing capability of a child is unquestionable. It is never too early to ensure that a child is parented the right way.

As this book unfolds, shades of some peculiar yet similar cases will meet the parents' eyes and hopefully will jolt them into realisation. I couldn't keep myself unfazed. Many cases were almost similar in nature. The origins of most of these problems could be traced to the parents' own weaknesses— anxiety, rigidity, anger and indiscipline.

Parents!

The keys to your child's locked unknown futures lie within yourself. It is essential to make a start today to ensure your child's bright tomorrows.

Children look up to their parents as their role models. They are conditioned by their environment, and parents form a primary part of this milieu. Therefore, it is imperative as a parent to make sure you present the right image to your child, because a child, in a sense, is the father of the man, as originally pronounced by William Wordsworth.

Marriage is the oldest institution. And, in most homes, the fruitful culmination of marriage is considered to be the birth of a child. Childhood is a very important stage in one's life since all-pervasive developments take place during this period and personality starts taking shape. Parenting holds a significant place in determining a child's behaviour. Every facet of a child's behaviour bears some testimony to the manner in which he has been nurtured and nourished. Parenting style encompasses both psychological and social development of a child, which starts quite early. The parents' personality predicts parental communicative behaviour and the range of behaviour of their child.

When parents adopt a parenting style that is not conducive to the normal psychosocial growth of their children, it can lead to the development of behavioural problems in them. Child-rearing style is an important determinant of a child's cognitive and psychosocial development that finally guides his behaviour.

It is a common observation that many parents, driven by faulty self-perception (holding the notion that 'I am the one who is always correct'), impose inappropriate demands upon their children. This sends a wrong message to the children, and they end up perceiving their parents negatively. Thus, problems in children seem to be determined by the dynamics of parent-child interaction.

Personality traits of the parents and the parenting style they adopt could have a profound impact on their child-rearing practice; and it is the mother who plays a crucial role in the rearing process of the child. Hence, personality characteristics are considered to be important aspects which influence one's perception of life's experiences and are the primary parameters of the strength or weakness of parents.

Good parenting is predominantly characterised by love, affection, care and encouragement, whereas negative parenting is characterised by discouragement, rejection, neglect, impositions and punishment. Communication between the parent and child enhances the quality of parenting. Since expression is the foundation of love, the importance of expressions assumes overriding priority.

Parental depression and anger are major causes for the development of problems in the children. In most of the cases that I have dealt, maternal depression and father's anger are the commonest factors in the development of behavioural problems in their child.

The anger and hostility levels could be quite high in the parents with the behaviourally disordered children. It is found that this repetitive cycle of anger is maintained in the children as they identify themselves with their fathers' temperament, which they incorporate in their own lives.

There are several parents who suffer from psychosomatic disorder due to their high anxiety and poor coping styles, which seem to be more threatening for a congenial family environment, and this prevents their child from establishing an emotional closeness with their parents.

Moreover, a number of parents revealed that due to their high anxiety state, they are prone to minimize the negative mental health (anxiety, depression, anger etc.) by being more extrovert (e.g., enjoyment seeking behaviour) because the need for affiliation, attention and fun can largely compromise the impact of negativity in them. It was a common observation through a number of cases that parents with higher anxiety often predispose themselves to experience joy and happiness by seeking excitement and stimulation from the outer world. This enjoyment includes cocktail party, intimate relationship with the opposite sex, attraction towards alcohol; shopping mania, kitty party, gambling, betting, some other exciting and thrilling behaviour (net-surfing, remaining busy with social media). Perhaps, this makes them ego-centric and turns their attention to their own need-satisfaction and enjoyment even at the cost of interpersonal relationship, when it is not relevant to their pleasure, right at that moment. This behavioural trend of parents appears to be detrimental to the development of a positive perception of the child for her parents—no matter how much luxury and comfort they provide for their family. Their emotional aloofness towards their child suggests that the parents' giving priority to interpersonal intimacy, preference for other people, and tendency to experience joy and happiness of their own could not be appreciated by the child. A child who is silently perceiving the parents with indifference and negligence has nothing to say and she makes her own world inwardly without understanding her parents or what is going on in their mind.

Thus, the parents' characteristics of high anxiety and enjoyment-seeking nature, resembling the externalised pattern of behaviour, may play a critical role in shaping a child's behaviour in the same direction.

A child appreciates and wants to see his parents as caring and interested in, spending maximum time with him and sharing their feelings and experiences with him; but the parent's own issues, problems and enjoyment-seeking nature overshadows the imperative need for providing the child with loving and rewarding experiences.

Thus, the discrepancy between the children's needs and desires, on the one hand, and the parent's capability to cater for, on the other, constitutes a burning issue which should be resolved as soon as possible.

Since the mother stands as a big source of emotional and psychological strength for her child, the absence of the perception of positive feelings could induce unpleasant feelings and stress in the child. The child's perception of his mother as protecting, rewarding and non-neglecting implies that the positive personality characteristics in the mother makes the child feel protected, rewarded and less neglected. Hence, the mother is perceived as dependable. This gives rise to a good relationship with the child's perception of the mother as protecting and caring. This positive notion of the child makes him proud to identify himself with the mother and to feel motivated to internalise the given social values and norms.

Marriage is one of the life's most significant, and in many ways, difficult responsibilities. It has, and makes, its own demands. A spouse, when unable to cope with the stresses of his/her marital life, develops unhealthy habits and qualities, and this has far-reaching consequences for everyone involved.

Gender bias exists. It is very much a fact. However, it is imperative that this should not disturb the harmony of a family. Men and women have certain distinct traits, characteristic reactions, differences in thoughts and actions. It is important for a couple to recognise these differences, work towards a compromise and to weave their disparate schools of thoughts into a single, synchronised fabric of a balanced family life.

So, parents have to understand how the chaotic environment of the home due to parental poor adjustment and constant quarrel may fill a child with aggressive tendencies, inculcate a sense of fear and nurture hatred towards them. Security, reinforcement and attachment, three major determinants of a pleasant life, are adversely affected in a child in association with parental discord and maladjustment. This makes them hungry to get stimulation to fill their sense of emptiness owing to the absence of secure attachment with such a significant person in life. As a result, she becomes the victim of either externalized (aggressive) behaviour or internalized (depressive) behaviour as a way of compensatory behaviour.

Thus, depression, anxiety, excitement-seeking behaviour, and maladjustment of parents set a model for the child to observe and learn socially inappropriate behaviour and assimilate it with her own. This learnt and acquired behaviour of a child gradually becomes a part of her own personality. The need for attachment is not restricted to early age only, it continues in adulthood, too. Therefore, a child needs love and affection, off and on, even in adulthood.

It can be easily imagined that a child's maladaptive behaviour, due to unhealthy socialization, is the outcome of her adaptation to a distorted family atmosphere imparted by the parents, and the poor quality of parenting.

I start my journey into the human mind with the hope of parents' introspection about themselves and the events with an intention to rectify the unpleasant happenings.

Parents, are the best persons to identify their problems. Here is a checklist:

- ☐ Have you been experiencing anxiety?
- ☐ Are you under stress?
- ☐ Do you find yourself to be inflexible and rigid on various issues?
- ☐ Do you have anger issues?
- ☐ Are you rigid and indisciplined in your personal life?
- ☐ Do you find that your own childhood was unpleasant?
- ☐ Do you have a difficult married life?
- ☐ Do you consider yourself as an incompetent parent?
- ☐ Are you aware of your temperament and perception of your true self?
- ☐ Do you know that your child perceives you differently?

And so I decided to embark on a journey to discover the roots of the differences arising within a family by assessing the cases related to parent-child issues.

❑❑❑

PART-I

Parents' Planet

- *Parental issues that affect a child*
- *Problem areas and solutions to resolve them*

Wait, Watch Yourself
Before Disciplining Your Child

ANXIETY

In today's world, anxiety is a normal phenomenon. But if parents habitually look tense and behave irrationally, that is not normal, and certainly not in the eyes of their child.

Overanxious parents are often prone to have rigid and anger-linked temperaments. The rigidity and anger in them are the expressions of their own deep-rooted anxieties and insecurities. As frustrations accentuate, they indulge in, or fall prey to different kinds of addictions and psychological diseases, like, depression and other ailments. The addictions and psychological problems of an individual are clearly correlated to one's own temperament.

Let us find out how parental anxiety takes the shape of rigidity and anger which becomes a big cause for their own destruction. Ultimately their children are the sole sufferers.

Dear Parents! You must learn to check your own anxiety.

Now, let us analyze the possible causes of one's problems realistically one by one.

To check why you are anxious, find out the areas which bother you frequently and put a tick mark in the box (√):

Are you anxious because of the following?

- ☐ Your child's academic record is not up to your expectations.
- ☐ You are burdened with your financial insecurity.
- ☐ You have your professional issues.
- ☐ You have your personal issues.
- ☐ You are unable to fulfil your child's demands.
- ☐ You are unable to spend adequate time with your child.
- ☐ You are worried about the issue of your child's pocket money.
- ☐ You are upset with the complaints from the school teachers about your child's misbehaviour.
- ☐ Your child's television, facebook and mobile addiction make you agitated.

- [ ] You find that your child's friends' circle is really worrying.

If parents can identify the causes of their anxiety, the battle is won because then, they can go ahead with solving these issues. Their maturity makes them stand tall even in the face of the most challenging or demanding situations. It happens when they carry conviction that, every problem has a solution.

To begin with, let us take a close look at the dynamics in a family and how even trivial issues might affect other factors, even though on the surface they seem completely unrelated. So, it is not the child to blame but the parents, who need a lot of effort to correct themselves.

As this book unfolds, shades of some peculiar, albeit singular cases, will catch the readers' eyes, and hopefully stir them up to take corrective steps. This is why, I decided to inquire into parents' own problems before dealing with the ones of their children.

Now it is your turn to analyse the problems which are detrimental to your child.

For instance, notice how parents behave in the following situations:

Academic competition is becoming tougher day by day, and parents increase children's stress by imposing their own anxiety on them. Be a supportive parent. Parents emotional support will give them tremendous courage to perform to their utmost potential.

There is the case of an eleven-year girl, named Lisa, with her extreme reaction after her poor performance which compelled her towards an attempt to commit suicide, which I want to share with you.

Lisa, after getting her report card and finding she had scored low marks in some subjects, ran away from school. She broke down before me, crying inconsolably. She told me that she wanted to commit suicide and was at a loss how to do it. Fortunately, a benevolent person was suspicious about her and could understand her intention. He talked to her and found that his guess was true and he consoled her and brought her home.

The worried parents contacted me. The surprising element to convey is that her parents were absolutely unaware of the fact that their own expectations led their child to take such a drastic step.

They admitted that they often wanted their child to achieve high marks and she was capable as well. Lisa was popular among her friends' owing to her good results. Their expectations might have had a role which motivated her to secure good marks.

This is a clear-cut picture of the parent's own anxious state, which is here reflected in their child's academic performance. The child develops a fear of withdrawal of love if she doesn't perform well. Moreover, she was quite worried about her parents because they always talked to the relatives about their daughter's performance. This created profound anxiety in her mind. She was feeling guilty as she could not come up to her parents' expectation. As a result, she wanted to finish herself off. This stressful situation kept her always in a state of despondency.

There are several Lisas and their parents who are going through similar tremendous inner conflicts. On the one hand, a child is ashamed of facing his parents and, on the other hand, the parents fear disgrace ahead of them.

See how Julia used to comfort her daughter, Penny, who was about to appear at her school final examinations, saying things like,

"Don't get panicky darling, relax! What a person needs are a beautiful mind and a charming personality. And you possess both. After finishing your examinations you've to show your efficiency in every walk of your life."

She used to assert before her that the school final examination was as easy and simple as other school examinations. Penny was quite confident and positive. She has now made a good career and secured a high post in a prestigious multinational company. She is there not due to the high achievement/or score in her school but her dynamic and determined attitude towards life and her capability to face its challenges. Education and marks are two different dimensions. Education enriches one's outlook whereas high score limits one's knowledge up to the book only.

The 'high scoring' culture is prevalent in our society to a great extent as if this was a brownie point in one's curriculum vitae. In fact, if you go through the records of successful persons you will find that most of them were average achievers in their class performance. There is a huge difference between the class performance and a child's ability to go ahead in life. So, academic achievements are no indicator of one's ability to establish oneself in a desired place. Education is a form of culture. It enriches a child's knowledge. Education helps inculcate discipline.

Study should be enjoyable. A child should be curious about the subjects. Parents should serve up education as a delicacy. Do not make it bitter or sour. Unfortunately, parents, now a days are missing the actual significance of education. So, parents, Be logical!

Mark Twain may have rightly said, I have never let my schooling interfere with my education.

A child needs emotional support. Every child is different and he perceives his parents differently. So the habit of study differs from one to another. But the technique and mechanisms are universal. A child with stress is unable to receive the information related to studies. He needs a stress-free environment so that he can store the learnt items comfortably and easily in his memory-compartment and can recall it without hassles. He just hates it if his parents talk about his studies, performance etc., so he starts rebelling against the parents' expectations or their boasting of his performance. But this rebellion takes many forms from depression to aggression. People with a lot of anxiety often ignore the feelings and sensitivity of their children which arise as a consequence of their own temperament. A child cannot have an omniscient view. They cannot adjust themselves to their studies while facing such parental problems. If you perceive your child's problems by considering them from the viewpoint of a third person, you will find it easier to identify the problems they encounter every day.

Parents with successful children are very systematic, organised and understand the values of education and its importance. The following example proves how parents make studies easy and comfortable by proving that Education is a culture.

"It was the system of my home to sit and practise anything related to studies, like when she was three years old she had to sit exactly at 6'o clock in the evening. Since she was very young we used to give her freedom to learn rhymes and identify colours or use chalks or crayons for drawing meaningless things. We (mother and father) divided this duty and made it compulsory. When she was a kid we had to sacrifice some of our household works. We didn't have time to decorate our home, attend parties, get involved in kitty parties, or cook a variety of things every day. But we used to participate with her in her studies, extracurricular activities and school functions. Now I'm feeling so good that she takes her own initiative and is performing well in her class and even in extracurricular activities." Thus, if you take care of your child from the beginning you need not worry about his future.

Financial insecurity is faced by a number of people. Anxiety on such issues should not affect parents at the expense of their child's mental or psychological state.

There is the case of Rohit, a nine-year-old boy. He came with his parents and appeared overburdened with a weight he found hard to bear. His eyes were full of tears as if someone had punished him. His dejected mood was the cause of his parents' concern, which brought him to me.

The parents' complaint was — "He never seems to be happy. He doesn't talk to us. He doesn't want to go anywhere. His academic record was good; but now it's dropping day by day. We have no clue where things went wrong."

This case revealed that the parents themselves were very sad about Rohit's worsening academic performance. Rohit, who used to score brilliantly, was suddenly undone by their high expectations.

Rohit briefed me that he was not able to face academic competition as his parents often talked about his performances with their relatives. But he was more anxious about his father's financial limitations and the expenditure on his education. He also confided in me his fear that if he did not get good marks he will certainly feel ashamed and cannot forgive himself as his father was spending a lot of money on his tuitions and school fee, despite their financial constraints. Moreover, he was very sensitive to the quarrelling of his parents inter se on financial issues, which left him with the disconcerting sensation that a large amount of money was being spent on his studies.

During the interaction with the parents it was revealed that they had no idea that their repeated mention of 'excessive money' being spent for the child's education had made him anxious and robbed him of his confidence out of fear of failure.

However, owing to the parents' ignorance or their insensitivity, that they were unaware that the reaction of their child towards their financial problems might be responsible for his low spirits and sadness. In fact, a child keeps a sharp eye around the home environment and he dissects the situations with his own perspective. A child has his independent unique perception of many things which a parent hardly comprehends.

Thus Rohit may realise their sacrifices and try his best to reach his parents' expectations but with an uncertainty and disturbed mind: would he be able to do that? This factor induced stress and fear in him.

If a parent is going through a financial crisis or if he is not financially strong, he should not express his sacrifices to his child. Such an expression would simply suggest as though a parent was obliging his child which makes him more vulnerable to stress.

Saumya's father had limited earning. He was trying to provide the best education to his daughter. Saumya has learnt that her parents are often happy and encouraging. They never showed any negative gesture to their daughter. As a result, Saumya never felt that her parents were under financial stress, although she knew the reality. Her demand was less and she used to study on her own. She was regularly attentive in her class and was invariably listening intently to the teachers while learning lessons. Due to her parents' happy-go-lucky temperament she could forget the poverty and so called recreations.

You are unable to fulfil your child's demands.

In several cases, it is found that parents are worried about their inability to fulfil the demands made by their children. The parents' own anxiety and frustrations may make the home environment depressing.

"It's not possible for me to provide my child with readymade food. When his friends have this he easily gets upset and demands junk food or money...and junk foods are so expensive...we can't afford them." This is a common problem faced by parents. The junk food in varieties of eye-catching packets (chips etc.) are becoming popular day by day; a child gets attracted easily and wants to have them immediately. Many parents adopt this culture like a 'status-symbol' and take it as if it were their prestige issue if they did not buy the junk foods in loads. This makes them compulsive buyers.

On the other hand, parents who are financially incapable have guilty feelings because they are not able to fulfil their child's desires. Fulfilling a child's demand is a critical issue now. Parents who are already sad, because they are not able to fulfil their child's demands, should not be all the more unhappy, for there are ways to solve any problem.

Parents who spend a lot of money on such things to make their child temporarily happy may have to face different kinds of problems when he grows up. His demands will increase from minor to major. They have to be careful while fulfilling the demands. Moreover, their child develops an unhealthy food habit. In this connection, a case in point is the habit of taking fast food, which, if not checked, may cause ill-effects on the child's health. Surprisingly, I found that very few parents are worried about the concept of healthy food. Eating out in hotels and restaurants and the readymade-food culture are coming up so strongly that parents begin to develop an inferiority complex if they fail to follow this new trend. The parents' own complex has a definitive effect on their child.

How to solve the problem

Notwithstanding this, it is unfair to stop or quarrel over the issue of a child's desire to have junk food. If parents object or show their incapacity to buy, they may induce an inferiority complex in their child because it is a natural demand from a child. It is advisable to adopt a good as well as a healthy method to fulfil his desires. Thus either providing in excess, or depriving a child of the item for which he has a craving induces unhappiness in him and, ultimately, he may try to get the things by hook or by crook.

Parents can cultivate a good habit in their child by making a healthy rule. They can fulfil the demand of their child on every weekend with a condition attached that he has to have regular healthy food on weekdays. Here, parents can control their feelings of guilt, and a child also learns to have good healthy food. Here the 'junk food' becomes an incentive or game as a reward, with a health condition attached, only if they have 'healthy food' six days in a week.

It is almost impossible to stop a child's natural urge to have junk foods but, at the same time, one can balance it by being more logical and rational. This is the easiest way to solve this problem and make a child happy and healthy. Moreover, it also teaches a child how to develop patience.

You are worried over the issue of your child's pocket-money.

Mayank, has been very restless, disobedient and argumentative from his childhood. Moreover, his stealing habit made his parents more aggressive, rather than worried. Despite being the son of a rich father, he hardly got pocket money. As a result, he started stealing money whenever he got the chance. His parents started treating him like a thief. Their abusive language and corporal punishment made their son more rigid. He began taking revenge on his parents by being adamant and destructive. He formed a tendency to run away from home and spend the night with his friends of the same mindset. His stealing tendency got so aggravated that he ended up by being a real thief, in terms of stealing and forcing his parents to hand over money to him as much as he required. Now he is nineteen years old and he spends most of his time with his friends either in a club or recreation centre, and testing his fate in gambling and betting. Now he needs money for fulfilling his destructive needs.

Teach your child the value of money.

Many parents do not realise that spending money is one of the major social needs of a human being and it is normal for their child to develop and express a burgeoning curiosity in financial matters. So parents should accept this fact and try to satisfy their child's curiosity. They should teach him how to handle money. They must keep this in mind: the sooner the better! They should give up the erroneous notion: it is too early to teach the child about money matters.

The best way to teach your child economics and finance is to spend money through him. Educating children about money teaches them how to be immune to the lure of money.

It is very much advisable to provide the child with certain small responsibilities related to the handling of money, for example, letting him pay the fare, pay the staff etc. Money in his hands makes him a confident and trustworthy child and increases his mental skills and sense of social responsibility as well. It also subsides the greed for money.

Here is an example of happy and proud parents.

Meghna has such parents who are not only educated but also have a broad and sensible outlook towards life. They used to give their daughter some amount of money whenever they went on trips and encouraged her to pay for everything, e.g., for shopping bills and fares and also pay for other commodities right from when she was six years old. They decided to give her some pocket money when she was ten. They made it a point for her to spend it as she liked, but her small necessities like pencil, eraser, etc., were also included in that expenditure. When she grew up they increased the amount of money by inclusion of her mobile charges, internet services and so on. If she exceeded the fixed amount, it was going to be her own problem because the extra amount would be deducted from the following month's pocket money; thereby, she slowly developed the sense of responsibility and learnt the true value of money.

In fact, a child who starts handling money earlier has not much curiosity and does not have greed towards money. But the deprived child, who faces problems and pressure due to money, develops lots of behavioural problems, like stealing, lying, aggression, or nurturing a revengeful attitude.

You are unable to spend adequate time with your child.

Inability to spare time is becoming a challenging issue day by day for both parents. It is becoming tougher as both parents are working. They are more insecured, nurturing a sense of guilt and reactive at the same time. These negative feelings are so strong in them that they spoil the given time by being more anxious, depressed or hostile. They are big failures in managing their child-related activities and spending enough time because they waste their leisure time on grumbling. They lack the insight and have no practical knowledge of QUALITY TIME.

Let's see how Honey, a mother of seven years old son, proves herself a good mother.

Honey is working in a multinational company. Her style of rearing her son may provide some guidelines to parents who are often in a state of anxiety and are grumpy.

Honey comes back from office at 5 O'clock in the evening, kisses her seven-year-old son, prepares tea and snacks, of course, the menu is prefixed, because she cannot afford to waste her time in deciding the stuff. She takes a newspaper and starts solving jumbles with the help of her son, as if her son is teaching her. They consult a dictionary if they fail to find some words; of course, Honey does it intentionally so that her son takes more interest in this game. She tries to lose the game, in order to make her son win deliberately. She spends only fifteen minutes on it, for the sake of her son's personality and skill-development. This is called quality time, and, at the same time, the child is learning by playing and that too, with his mother. Now she starts her regular activities, including her son's routine-studies. These precious moments with her son stand out as 'positive-participation' with him.

You are upset with the complaints from teachers about your child's misbehaviour in the school.

The parents of Naman (ten year old) were terribly upset to hear about the complaints, regarding their son which they had never dreamed of and reacted as if it was a nightmare. The following was the list of complaints causing disturbance to the whole class—

1. Aggressive (beats, kicks and punches).
2. Teases the girl students.
3. Steals money from other students' bags.
4. Makes bad gestures even in front of his teachers.
5. No remorse or guilty feeling.
6. No respect towards school authorities.
7. Destroys school property, e.g., breaks black-board, chairs, table etc.

Naman's parents were completely clueless regarding Naman's violent and destructive nature. He was a totally different child at home. In his mother's words, "He never displays any indisciplined actions as our family maintains a strict family tradition which we are bound to follow. We don't allow any mischief or misbehaviour. So it's really a hard time for us to accept such bad and destructive behaviour. We were getting small complaints from the school previously and we had started working towards that being more strict. We even tried to punish him by being more vigilant. Sometime we used to deny him many things. But we couldn't understand that he could behave so badly...His father started beating him and we're also losing family prestige."

Listen, parents!

Naman's parents were absolutely correct in terms of the family values. But could they think of the problems where he was suffering every day by suppressing his natural needs and desires due to the disagreements and animosity of his parents?

Naman was not the only one who was suffering from deviant or undesirable behaviour, there are a good number of students who lack attention and are unable to maintain the societal norms. The child, like Naman, who was caged in his own home and lived in a state of constant fear of unpredictable behaviour of his parents, often has a tendency to boil with anger and is looking for the appropriate place and time to ventilate his deep-rooted aggression and hatred towards his parents. Because he wants to unload his gnawing feelings somewhere. So the school becomes the ideal place for him where he interacts with like-minded children and finds an opportunity to throw tantrums. He feels powerful by doing so.

Let us know about the root cause of such disturbing behaviour of children who constantly live in a state of fear that if they revolt against the parents they will strongly disapprove of his actions and he has no other place to go.

Parents, listen! Find the source of your child's pent-up emotions which give rise to his violent instincts and disturb the strategy of his own thought patterns.

When a child is being kept in a strict environment he develops hostility and hatred towards the authority figures (here, parents) because he cannot take revenge against such a significant person in his life. So the child comes to the school from his home with a bag full of aggression, hostility, ruthlessness, destruction, and pugnacity instead of bringing the texts. So his school bag becomes a Pandora's box, full of grief and anxiety. His grief and anxiety come in the form of aggression and destruction which become the symbol of his defiance..He feels satisfied and happy if he has fulfilled his tasks by taking revenge on his parents by destroying school property and beating other students. This sense of accomplishment motivates him to go ahead in his life, in order to defend himself from nurturing pain, frustration and depression.

Naman's parents blamed the school authorities and their child's peer groups because they did not realise that they were at fault. They had been maintaining the same methodology or system in the house for decades.

In fact, a child needs an environment where he can feel free to interact with his age-related developments and the parents are the only important persons who can listen to his problems patiently and help him grow in the right direction. Their self-made ideology needs a change for the welfare of their own progeny.

Deb, a seven year old child, confided in me, "While I was punching Manas (a child of the same class), I was imagining that I was punching my father...my dad pushed me out of the room because I could not complete my school work...look at my arm! I got the injury because my dad pushed me hard...so I start beating them (friends) because of my dad..."

He was so scared of narrating his wished-for aggression towards his father even though his father was not present there at that time. Because the counselling was being conducted in one of the school premises which was completely isolated. He was looking at my eyes with full confidence but an obvious fear was there when he asked,

"So you're not going to tell him?..."

There are innumerable factors which make parents anxious. Parents' anxiety needs a channel through which it can pass. There are always problems in life. The important thing is to solve them rationally. A parent who is preoccupied with his/her own anxiety tends to inculcate poor discipline in his/her child. So their first duty is to set free from their own anxiety.

RIGIDITY

Anxiety often takes the shape of rigidity. A person with an anxious state of mind often denies changes out of fears. The state of insecurity turns into rigidity.

Rigidity, at a fundamental level, is not a bad characteristic. But when it becomes suffocating for others, well, you need to be wary about it. Rigidity is a trait which has detrimental effects on the stability of one's family.

To check if you are a RIGID person, assess the following statements; when you say YES, put a tick mark in the box (√):

1. ☐ Do you think it is hard for you to enjoy in different situations?
2. ☐ Do you become angry when you find a new item in your plate?
3. ☐ Do you find yourself less curious?

4. ☐ Do you become angry when your orders are not carried out by your family members at once?
5. ☐ Do you stick to your opinion that television, computer or other electronic gadgets are a big hindrance to your child's development?
6. ☐ Are you inclined to say 'no' when your family wants to go with you on a pleasure trip?
7. ☐ Is it hard for you to change your plan for the convenience of your family?
8. ☐ Are you often adamant that 'eating-out' is just wastage of money?
9. ☐ Do you think others' suggestions are not worthwhile, and how often are you inclined to say 'no'?
10. ☐ Is it hard for you to accept the choices of your family, for your clothing?
11. ☐ You become angry when any change takes place in your working area, bedroom, and living room etc.
12. ☐ If others disagree with your opinion you try to convince them and if they are not convinced you dissociate yourself from them very easily.
13. ☐ Whatever you do or say, you want other people to perceive it in the same manner.
14. ☐ It is hard for you to accept a mistake or feel sorry.
15. ☐ You like people who often agree with you or your feelings.
16. ☐ You feel proud in being logical and rational most of the time.
17. ☐ It gives you a lot of stress while recalling the happenings of the day so you stop revisiting them out of fear.
18. ☐ You find it is really impossible to change your ways fearing it will cause another problem.
19. ☐ You often avoid reality by involving yourself in light tasks, like watching television, indulging in gossip, etc., which often divert you from stressful areas.
20. ☐ You often feel uncomfortable in seeking help from others.

The above statements reflect one's rigid attitudes. If most of your answers are in the affirmative, it goes to reflect your rigid personality in various aspects of your life. A person with this disposition becomes rigid even on minor issues in most of the cases.

All the above statements describe your strong likes and dislikes. A person with such a disposition may hold a fixed outlook towards every happening in one's life and follow it blindly.

Many a time, it is found that rigidity is the cause of **ego problems**.

"I have told her several times that I do not enjoy movies": a husband was complaining about his wife.

"I told her a number of times that eating out is just a waste of money. I cannot appreciate this planning so I can't involve myself. It doesn't suit me and my mentality how can anyone force me?"

"My husband never asks anything. He keeps silent most of the time. He is least interested in family affairs. How can I know what is going on within his mind? Even his lack of curiosity confused me many times": -a wife was expressing her views about her husband.

While talking to her husband he told me, "I don't need to know much about it. I know what's going on in my house and what's brewing in her mind."

Here, the rigidity in the husband shows his well developed 'ego'. Because he has already made it clear, now he cannot change his concepts.

This was the crux of the problem: husband's rigid way of family perception which blocked the way to new ideas, changes and views. In most cases, the situation worsens where both spouses are rigid. Thus, the rigidity in a person reflects his\her own insecurity and feeling of being powerful and dominating. His deep-rooted anxiety and insecurity gives him a false image of superiority and pride. He does not want to accept his own shortcomings. The need to be right is so much conspicuous in him as he has hardly a realization of being wrong.

The following case, where the mother is really worried about her ten-year-old son's stubbornness and tantrums, illustrates my observation that the merit of good habits in the incipient stage of childhood when learning is easy and long-lasting, is often ignored by parents. It is hard for parents to comprehend how they transfer to their child their own rigidity and tantrums in a subtle way:

Mother's complaint: I don't think I take any half measures in the care of my child. I wake up early in the morning, make his breakfast and pack lunch for him. Then I accompany him to the school-bus stop. I feel as if I was living only for my son. But still, his temper and tantrums stay with him—don't know why. He intentionally takes more time to get ready for school. He often teases me by wasting his time in brushing his teeth and taking a bath. I'm sure that if I do not scold him he will miss his school bus. Help me."

Child's complaint: "My mom always insists that I do just what she says. She allows me little or no space to do things on my own. Sometimes, she slaps me and scolds me a lot. I don't want to go to school because I feel bad."

Here, I found the mother was passing on her own rigidity to her son subtly, as if being adamant was the main strategy to get the desired work done.

The child eventually learns that parents' rigid behaviour can be effectively counteracted if he exercises power more vigorously than they are capable of doing out of natural power stemming in the childhood. The message the child gets for this behaviour originating from his mother is that the more powerfully one acts, the more likely one can overpower one's adversary.

The mother asked, "What to do under such circumstances where a child is not serious about the timings and the importance of school?"

The solution is as simple as the problem itself.

During the interview session, there emerged a few points worth noticing. To start with, the mother's attention was bordering on extra-caution. This would lead to interference in small and natural habits of the child. Her rigidity was thus making him an irritable child. Small acts ranging from putting paste on the toothbrush or tying shoelaces are what fascinate a kid. He loves making a game even out of petty affairs, and handles such little chores to that effect. Meddling with their state of activities peeves them no end, as is the case with this set of mother-child.

This is a significant negative trait which transfers from the parents to the child, and often affects a child in the long run with serious repercussions. Truly speaking, a number of parents who suffer from rigidity often have been victims of such rigidity in their own childhood environments, thus making them even more liable to fall into this trap. Parents who are on the verge of such a similar situation should be careful while handling such a delicate issue. Do you want to be the culprit behind the rigidity of your child?

So a child needs his own space and wishes to learn by himself. The duty of a parent is to design the timings and make a beautiful map for that with a warning that he has to complete the whole schedule within the time range. If he is unable to complete it, he is always welcome to ask for help.

Do not nag. You can make the map in the following manner:-

Fix the wake-up alarm.

Time for washing rituals, toilet, brushing-teeth, taking a bath, (15/20 minutes).

Putting on school uniform, shoes, etc. (5/7 minutes).

Breakfast (10 minutes) – including washing hand, beforehand and after breakfast.

*Remember, it is convenient to arrange the child's school bag every night before going to bed. Now your child is ready to leave.

The above chart will give an opportunity to a child to become independent and responsible. Parents should assure them that they are always ready to participate in his daily chores, to enable him to adhere to the time schedule if he really needs it.

Mom rigid!

The following case shows how a grown-up child becomes disobedient and stubborn by watching her role model's rigidity and anger from her early childhood to teen age.

Here, Emma, a sixteen-years-old girl, accompanying her mother, entered my clinic with the following loud conversation going on: (I was more interested in watching and listening than stopping them so that I would be able to draw some pictures regarding them.)

"...Yes mom! I don't want to stay with you. I'm looking for a paying guest accommodation." Emma sounded confident and decisive.

Her mother yelled, "How dare you! You are my daughter, you have to obey me. You've no right to take any decision unless and until you get married."

Emma was louder, "I don't deny I'm your daughter. But you can't control me. Look! I'm grown up now; you want to treat me as if I am your puppet from my childhood. Now those days are gone...I will do what I want...!"

There was a big verbal illogical battle ongoing between the two. They were accusing each other for small matters. Neither of them was ready to compromise.

Later, I learnt that Emma had run away from her house and taken shelter in her friend's house. Her friend informed her parents. They came and forcibly took her from her friend's house. Emma's complaint was that her mother always dominated her. She never allowed her to do anything of her own choice. She actually wanted to get free from the restrictions, not the parents.

Her mother was well qualified. It is a sad state of affairs and shocking to see educated mothers, like Emma's, behave irrationally with their daughters. Here, Emma represents the victim of the parents' own weaknesses—anxiety, rigidity, and anger which ended up in hers being the most undisciplined mother. Emma's demand was not acceptable—this is the true state of affairs. But the reason behind this demand is quite serious which made Emma take such a decisive step.

Her innocent eyes have some expression as if it was conveying: *Mom! What have you turned me into?*

I could read it.

Parents who are facing a similar situation should be careful while handling such a delicate issue.

You need to keep changing yourself continuously, in order to provide the right kind of parenting.

How to get rid of your rigid temperament?

Here are some tips which will enable you to be flexible.

TIPS FOR A RIGID PARENT:

- Communicate openly with everyone. This may reduce your rigidity and make you more open to change yourself.
- Perceive the world around you in an unbiased way. It may help you in becoming more flexible and adopting a new life-style.

- Exchange ideas with people around you. It will help you welcome other's ideas as well.
- Check your child's needs and desires. Do not be unreasonably adamant on issues which he considers to be important. After all, these are the natural demands of any normal, healthy child. Act with discretion!
- Don't always react with 'NO'. Make yourself available to understand your child's suggestions/demands. Let him know your opinions and ideas in a calm manner and explain why you disagree with him.
- If you do not like new food, try to taste its sample first and then express your feeling in a gentle manner so that your family can take care of your taste presently. Irritations on such a small thing may turn into a big crisis. Be soft-spoken, mild in your manners and flexible in your attitude as well.
- Curiosity regarding family happenings is a sign of concern. If you shut yourself up within yourself it either shows your low interest or your own preoccupation with ideas regarding the happenings. Be open!
- Electronic gadgets are good for anyone. Enjoy with your child and the gadgets in an appropriate manner and satisfy his curiosity up to some extent. It will make your child free to interact with you and also a healthy way for your child to access you whenever he finds himself in a dilemma. Be a supportive parent!

Remember: Change is the only constant in life.

ANGER

A rigid person wants everything in his own way. This rigidity, if left unchecked, can give rise to uncontrolled anger.

You are hardly aware of the fact that your child lies because he wants to protect himself from your anger. The worst-affected persons of your anger are your spouse and kids because they are close to your heart. Owing to anger, you end up severing a beautiful family bond and alienating yourself from the others. An angry person has no true friends.

Remember the maxim: Stone is heavy, sand is weighty; but a fool's wrath is heavier than both.

Try to bridge this gap! Anger is an expression of one's own inadequacies. And it is a clear evidence of a person's poor self-esteem. Managing one's anger is no big deal when one starts thinking in this direction.

In this context, I cannot help but sketch my personal experience. It was a time when I was visiting a friend's home. Her eight-year old son, Chikkoo, was enthusiastically serving me snacks from a plate. His mother, though, was afraid to let him do it, fearing he might break the expensive crockery. I was silently watching as this trivial issue snowballed into a major one. Suddenly, the boy dropped the plate, accidentally, of course. My friend flared up and gave her son a tight slap and ordered him to go to his room. This incident forced me to think: didn't my friend cause a loss of something much more precious than that plate—her son's self-confidence?

I was not surprised when my friend brought her son to my clinic after a few years. 'He has become a liar and a truant,'—his mother complained. I could surmise what, and who, made Chikkoo a problematic child.

Chikkoo is now fourteen years old. He told me. *"Initially I used to tell her the truth but her reactions do not allow me to tell anything to her now. She started insulting me before my playmates...I try to avoid her. I'm getting lots of problems in my school; instead of solving them she raises a storm ...Now I don't want to attend the classes. It's difficult for me to concentrate on my studies. As a result, my teachers, too, started scolding me...I want to stop my studies...It's not possible to be calm when my parents scold me on every petty issue...Where should I go? To whom shall I talk? It's hard for me to obey them. Their anger shut the door for me...for solutions to my problems. I bet! You can't change them, they are so rigid..."*

Anger represents the negative state of a person, and the victim of this anger tries to save himself by counter-reacting. Chikkoo's mother's anger stemmed from her rigidity. In trying to control Chikkoo's every single action, she had instead caused an emotional gulf to form between herself and her son. Her uncontrolled anger had compelled Chikkoo to turn against her and had led to a complete erosion of trust between the two.

Anger is not only harmful for a person who is its victim but it adversely affects everyone around him. When a person gets angry, he ceases to think rationally and fail to communicate clearly. If one becomes a slave to one's anger, one will end up losing the most prized possession: one's family.

Arjun, a twelve-year old boy, used to get complaints for his poor performance from his school, many a time. His parents were very upset. I found that his father had a very low level anger/patience threshold. He was constantly blaming his son and wife in his loud voice. His wife was trying to prove that her husband was the culprit behind Arjun's poor performance. He has anger issues. He wants everything should happen according to his ways and wishes; otherwise he would not hesitate to give vent to his anger.

Males adopt anger mechanisms to release their pent-up emotions. Regardless of that, this is most definitely a negative and unacceptable consequence.

Why is Dad angry?

- Males' ego gives them a false feeling of superiority, and presents them with an outlet to show off their masculinity. This is completely a self-made identity, which finds recognition no where.
- Masculinity—Men have an erroneous notion that anger is equivalent to masculinity. A man without anger is perceived as naïve and lack of such aggressive traits is wrongly designated as a feminine trait by their family members, friends, colleagues and sometimes even the very society in which they live. This is why men frequently regard any show of docility or calmness as a social stigma.
- Anger always showcases insecurity towards rejection. If a male concedes to a view point of his wife, he starts believing himself inferior to his wife. Thus, faced with this feeling of rejection, he tries to restore his own pride and demonstrate his own importance through anger and aggression.
- Dad has no time to let out his anger in a meaningful way, through playing sports, doing yoga or creative work. Therefore, the easiest way for him to release his stored emotions is through aggression as this requires no planning and effort and is easily expressed regardless of time and place.

Above all, anger has a genetic basis. It has been indicated in a lot of researches that anger often runs in those families where the grandfather or uncles reported this temperament. Anger in males is usually the result of the absence of a compliant role model, especially the father.

The worst form of anger is hidden anger. When dad remains silent and tight-lipped, concealing simmering anger inside him, it is a dangerous sign because such behaviour can be very unpredictable. His suddenly thrown tantrums often keep all the family members on their toes, such that they are forced to live in a constant state of fear. The children of such fathers keep a large distance from their fathers, fearing his actions which are imprudent, indiscreet and despicable. The Children who remain unsure about their fathers' actions and angry temperaments and are at a loss to explain them end up being confused and develop poor decision-making abilities. Thus they cannot distinguish between 'approved' and 'disapproved behaviour'.

Fathers! Your momentary outbursts may be the cause of permanent destruction of your family bonding. Learn to control your anger!

In the modern age there has come about a big revolution in the male school of thought. Men these days have developed new perspectives and respect for their female counterparts, and they are ready to bring about a radical change in their identities for the sake of the greater good. There are various avenues to reduce anger triggered by your own frustrations. Try the following methods:

TIPS FOR ANGER MANAGEMENT

Recollect and write down the reasons for your anger once a week.

- ☐ Is it related to your work place issues?
- ☐ Is it related to your financial problems?
- ☐ Is it related to your personal problems?
- ☐ Is it related to your child's poor academic performance?
- ☐ Is it related to your child's poor sense of discipline, such as, being a late-riser, lack of cleanliness and failure to maintain the schedule e.g., eating, studying, sleeping etc.

Now work out your problems.

If there is any problem related to work or financial troubles, it is advisable to share it with your spouse. You may include your child as well. You do not need to discuss the issue in detail. Just express anxieties which will help you in making your mood light and relaxed. This can also work as a stress-reliever. Moreover, if you have a small outburst, your family will understand and cooperate with you by keeping cool and quiet. After all, it is the family which is ready to support you emotionally.

Your personal problems may include various aspects: career and status competition, failure to meet the demands of your family, differences in opinions with your family members and many others. Your problem-solving attitude may be lower and your accumulated frustrations come out in the form of anger. The best thing is to sort out the problems one by one in an analytical way, instead of letting them fester stored in a mass. Think of whatever you have and do not get frustrated when you do not achieve the desired results. Think about those people who lack what you have. You will find many frustrations will disappear while thinking on these lines.

If your anger is related to your child's poor academic performance, before expressing it, you should find out the reasons. Those may have something to do with conflict within the family, problems with teachers or the peer group or the child's interest in another field, stream or subject, or they may be suffering from attention deficit disorder or other emotional problems.

Parents should be specific about the reasons behind their child's poor performance. If they detect the problem there is no point in getting angry. Because it is better to seek a solution to their child's problem with a cool mind. If a parent shows his temper he is certainly going to have a child with various kinds of behavioural problems.

Here, Emma's case may work as an eye-opener for parents. Her mother was so overbearing (rigid and angry) that she could not convince her daughter about her points of objection. However, the fact remains that Emma's mother loves her very much. She was excessively concerned over her security. What she told me cannot be ignored totally. The mother was filled with anxieties because her daughter was in her teens. She needed security. This was the reason behind her mother's excessively nagging nature. But she went on denying that her own behaviour towards her daughter was incorrect and her way of reacting wrong.

Anger is a form of emotion. Human beings with this instinct have natural outbursts. Anger happens when one loses control and it comes suddenly. In fact, it does not come in an organized way. Now this is the toughest question: how and when it should come.

Do you know the reasons for your outbursts? You do. But you never notice it. Most of the time, a person's anger is the result of his own pent-up feelings and piled-up frustrations. "Anger due to someone is expressed on someone else" is the commonest factor. This someone else is definitely your spouse and child. This is because you ignore any courtesy while dealing with them. But you often forget that even your family requires a parent with etiquette and manners while dealing with their innocent kids.

You have to take some time to ask yourself how to control your impulses.

Create some mental images of the events which are responsible for arousing your anger instinct. You will definitely find that there are a few issues which are intolerable and they occur repeatedly. As a result, you end up being the victim of your own anger. Now practise to overcome it. Find out from the following:-

- How your anger destroys the harmony of your home.
- How your child/spouse or other members of the family hesitate or stammer if you want to know the cause/reasons of any happenings.
- How they are forced to hide facts from you. Your anger makes them lie to you, in order to save themselves from your outbursts. Your child is the most innocent victim. His innocent mind now wanders and is busy thinking: how to make the excuses so that he can protect himself from your outburst.
- You have to be very careful about your angry outbursts; avoid projecting your anger on your loved ones. Your anger stems from deep-rooted insecurity and reveals your lack of self-discipline.

Remember: If you let your anger control you, you will end up alienating everyone around you.

However, anger is an instinct, an involuntary reaction, which you cannot stop totally.

Hence, follow faithfully the guidelines given below:-

Express your anger in a healthy manner. Suppression of anger is not only detrimental to your own emotional health but it may also lead to heart attack, diabetes or other physical ailments, including life-style diseases.

Let it out in an appropriate way, as Aristotle said:

'Anyone can become angry—that is easy, but to be angry with the right person, to the right degree, at the right time, for the right purpose, and in the right way—this is not easy.'

So anxiety, rigidity and anger are the expressions of parents' own insecurity and vulnerability to stress. If they accept their shortcomings and determine to check their temperaments, then only can they have a healthy and happy family.

When Anxiety starts Dominating You

Anxiety may become a big hindrance to your good parenting style. In most of the cases maternal depression and father's anger are the commonest factors responsible for ruining the peace and happiness of a family—I drew the conclusion by handling numerous parent-child problems. Anxiety and aggression in parents end up in their being "poor self-disciplined models" for their children.

Remember, parental anxiety and anger breed low self-esteem, feelings of insecurity and insufficiency in their child.

SPOT YOUR ANXIETY AND ITS INFLUENCE ON YOU

People with a lot of anxiety often ignore the sensitivity and feelings of their child which arise as a consequence of their own temperament. A child cannot have an omniscient view. He cannot adjust to his studies while simultaneously facing parental problems. If you perceive your child's problems by considering them from the viewpoint of a third person, you will find it easier to identify the problems he encounters every day.

HOW STRESS UPSETS YOUR INNER MECHANISMS

An anxious person often lives in a regime of constant tension, worry and uneasiness.

He is oversensitive in interpersonal relationships and frequently considers himself unequal to the tasks, and gets depressed easily.

- His decision-making tendency is low and poor. Every time he takes a decision he becomes tense and worries constantly if he has taken a wrong decision. Sometimes he seeks reassurance from other people.
- He often suffers from loss of sleep (insomnia) because he is prone to review all his events in his leisure time in a negative perspective. He blames himself or others even for minor mistakes. Ultimately, he spends sleepless nights and becomes the victim of depression.
- A depressive person often either detaches himself from others or being irregular at his normal activities, faces lots of personal, familial and social problems.
- He lacks problem solving and conflict management skills.

WHY DOES THIS HAPPEN?

Actually, intense fear is quite often related to one's faulty learning or conditioned fears which one might have gone through during one's childhood. The disturbed adjustment patterns of one's own parents might have had a great impact on one. Thus, fear may be the absorbed results of prior trauma of a parent.

If a parent does not confront his areas of problems and fears, he is very likely to develop a tendency to avoid the feared situations and stresses by developing various psychosomatic (mind and body) problems and personality disorders. He becomes prone to try and gain sympathy, excessive attention and meaningless support from others in order to escape from his own personal or official responsibilities. This adopted behaviour makes his life miserable which has a terrible impact on the family.

Obsession:

Revathi, a mother of 2 children 9 & 13 years, was looking desperate & confused due to her washing-rituals. She used to spend so much time on washing rituals that she had hardly any time to 'supervise' her children.

Let us know about the problems of Revathi, who represents several mothers trapped in more or less similar 'rituals'.

Infact, this state is known as obsession (frequent 'specific' thought) which easily turns into actions, known as compulsion. In the term of psychology it is known as obsessive-compulsive disorder.

Thus obsession is an irrational thought process whereas compulsion compels a person to perform the obsessed thoughts.

This manifests itself in different forms: clinging repeatedly to a fear-inducing thought which consumes one in its entirety or being completely fixated on a certain irritant to the pitch of irrationality. These traits are easily visible in one's behaviour (repeatedly washing hands, cleaning, counting numbers, checking locks, touching anything, etc.). Generally it does not have much effect on his normal performance.

A person with obsessive-compulsive traits unknowingly gets trapped in his own biases and prejudices ignoring the logical perspective of the problems, issues and its solutions.

An obsessive parent is so much obsessed with his own ideas, thoughts and actions that he hardly has time to supervise his child. Thus, the parents who themselves lack the quality of self-supervision are less efficient in supervising and monitoring their own child.

The effect of supervising and monitoring style of parenting is quite evident in the form of the parents' reduced warmth and greater hostility towards their child. It is advisable for parents to check their obsessive thoughts and compulsive actions. Obsession often turns into rigidity. It reflects one's inability to meet the demands of other people. As a result they often become prone to be either depressive or impulsive.

PSYCHOSOMATIC DISORDER

'Psycho' refers to one's mind and 'Somatic' refers to one's body.

Psychosomatic disorders may be acquired and maintained for a long time. These disorders are arising due to the arousal of emotional tension in response to stress situations.

Arousal of emotions influences the autonomic nervous system of human beings. Controlled emotions can control some of the responses voluntarily.

Parents who are depressed, find themselves helpless in solving the problems around them and want to escape from their responsibilities; more often they take the help of psychological mechanisms by adopting the various diseases which are broadly known as psychosomatic disorder.

If one stays in a state of depression or anxiety for a considerable period, one will certainly start showing the signs of physical illness which has its roots in one's psyche. So people should be careful and well informed so that they can diagnose their illness and be their own doctor.

A number of health problems from mild to severe, like headache, ulcers, migraine, high blood-pressure, heart-attack, even asthma (Coleman, Abnormal Psychology and Modern Life, 1988) are highly related to emotional reactions and mainly governed by one's psychological state.

STAY COOL: CHECK YOUR PULSE!

Have a look at how chronic emotional stress becomes the reason for a physical illness:

Headache and Migraine

Due to emotional stress muscles surrounding the skull contract and, as a consequence of these contractions, headache occurs. This pain recurs periodically at times of stress. So a person becomes restless and tends to take the help of medication without evaluating or reducing his cause of stress. So do not panic! Assess your problem carefully and discover the ways to get out of it.

Peptic ulcer

Worries, anger, anxiety, resentment and other negative emotional state may stimulate the flow of stomach acids beyond what is needed for digestion. If a person stays in stress for a long time the excess digestion acids may eat into the gastric linings and cause ulceration. Do not rush to doctor; examine the problems and check your stress.

Asthma

In some cases, asthma is considered to be associated with severe stress disorder. A person with asthma often fails to establish good interpersonal relationships and is also prone to failure in handling emotional issues. It is always advisable to find out the root cause of the stress. Because several accumulated and shocking stresses may cause an asthma attack. Deal with it with the help of a reliable person.

Hypertension

The heart is the most sensitive organ to get affected by emotional stress. Most people show alterations in blood pressure under stress. Thus high risk of developing chronic hypertension takes place when a person is under stress or sustained stress.

Heart attack

It is related to the incidence of loneliness, sleep-disturbances, nervousness, anxiety, depression, excessive working hours, and failure in achieving life's goals, problems related to family or other emotional issues. People with diabetes and high blood pressure often face silent heart-breaking problems due to their sensitivity to stress and inability to share stress and anxiety. Mostly introverted people decline to share their problems with others. It is essential for them to identify the underlying causes of their hypertension and diabetes, in order to save themselves from great loss.

Psychosomatic disorders cover a wide range of disturbances in which life-stress plays a causal role. Thus anxiety, rigidity, anger and indiscipline suggest complex personality characteristics due to the impact of negativity on a person.

Vinny, mother of two teen-age sons, says "I often feel sleepy. Whenever I start working I feel I am going to fall down. My heart starts palpitating violently. I'm not able to take care of my family. I know my children feel neglected but they manage themselves". There are many such cases where parents feel really helpless. Admittedly, the children cultivate a sense of self-reliance and enjoy the confidence of the parents.

Parents with this kind of history require positive insight and reasoning which enable them to solve their problems skilfully. Generally, parents who possess low determination and are poor in problem-solving skill, become the victims of many self-induced ailments. Such parents are unable to devote any time towards their children, and, therefore, a number of children who are suffering from many psychological and emotional problems have parents who belong to this category.

Vinny's 16-years-old son spends his time with his large group of friends—busy in drinking, smoking and gambling. Vinny has no clue about it.

Rozi is incapable of taking care of her 13-year-old daughter because she is herself a victim of self-created illness. Her daughter has been molested several times.

Zena suffers from migraine quite often and is unable to take proper care of her sixteen-year old child who looks sad, neglected, and rejected due to her mom's indifference. "I want to finish my life...My father keeps quiet…My mom is often in bed …I've none…with whom will I share my persistent feelings and problems?"

I was quite surprised to see tremendous changes in Vinny, Rozi and Zena. They are now fully recovered and completely free from the ailments which plagued them, and have become sincere and responsible mothers. They were so ashamed of themselves when they realised that their ignorance had played a major role in the destruction of their children that they instilled within themselves the resolve to work past their problems and take care of their children. They did not need to take any medication and it was only through determination and will power that they did wonders to their physical and psychological health.

DETERMINATION

Remember, constantly dwelling on your own problems is the biggest sin you can commit against your family. Neglecting your child is as big a crime as any on earth.

Now look at the following things which will allow you to work past your self-inflicted problems:

- Talk to your child regularly.
- Check his school bag, note book, diary etc., everyday.
- Keep his clothes, bed and room clean and encourage him to assist you.
- Provide him with good food.
- Check his home work and school work and guide him in whatever little way you can.
- Talk to his school friends and their parents as well.
- Make sure you develop familiar relations with the parents of his friends.
- Allot some time to talk to him about his friends, events and experiences in school.
- Enjoy shopping with him, having ice cream and watching movies.
- Your teenage child needs your guidance, love, and a friendly approach; and also a little bit of space.
- Take part in his hobbies and interests, and try to encourage them.
- The best way to be friendly with your growing child is to invite his friends occasionally and make them feel at home, irrespective of their gender.

- Discussing and sharing general knowledge with your child makes your child as well as you more educated and knowledgeable.
- Read the newspaper with your child.
- Solve puzzles and word jumbles with your child.
- With grown-up kids, you should share feelings and take suggestions on trivial and non-trivial issues.
- Involve him in financial strategy, home expenditure, savings, banking, paying bill etc.
- Enjoy cooking and experimenting with new recipes.
- Make sure when your child comes home during the vacations you can spare some exclusive quality time for him.

Once you start doing all of this, think about the time you have left in your day. Don't you start to think that you are running short of time? With such a shortage of time, how can you afford to fall prey to any self-inflicted illness? Remember, if you devote your time and efforts to your children it will pave the way for a healthy reciprocal relationship in your family.

Ironically, only parents who want to escape from all of the above responsibilities have a tendency to fall sick very easily. It is your turn to JUDGE yourself.

The best way to mirror you through your notebook (Annexur-I)

The good way to come out of your own problems is if you maintain a diary or a notebook of your own problems and your unorganized behavioural pattern, and you realise how it has affected your family, and see it once in a month. It will give you a bird's-eye view of ways to understand yourself and how your problems affect or influence you.

Think precisely and try to answer the following questions

- Why do you lose your temper?
- What motivates you to perform the actions you do?
- Why do you find difficulty in adjusting?
- Why do you insult your spouse and kids in front of your friends and staff?
- Why do you keep silent when you are supposed to share your views and opinions that are essential to keep your family together?

These activities sound very simple and part of the normal happenings of life. When we behave in a certain way, perform an action, or react to a stimulus, it seems right from our viewpoint because we hardly tend to assess or check our normal behaviour. But we scarcely give importance to the impact of our behaviour or reactions on our child.

You can minimise the chances of being the victim of innate negative traits (anxiety, anger and rigidity) and mitigate the effect on the child who is the victim of your way of treatment if you visualize your problems and inherited weaknesses. Each person is unique and has a different way of coping. If you spend some time in analysing and comprehending the situations, you may enjoy a wonderful family atmosphere.

Parents!

You will find a miraculous change in yourselves when you find out the cause of your own behavioural problems. Your way of communication is a reflection of your true self. The problems in rearing your child will soon disappear when you find yourselves in a good state of mind.

TIPS FOR ANXIOUS PARENTS:

Identify your general problems and apply effective methods of coping with them:

- Look for some time to sort out your painful thoughts. Quiet moments can give you clarity of thought and answers to some gnawing questions.
- Do not bury yourself in corner. Come in contact with reality.
- Discriminate between real and imagined threatening situations.
- Write about your persistent fear of situations which you may perceive in a magnified way and react to irrationally and you want to avoid it.
- Modify conditions in your life situations which are responsible in eliciting maladaptive behaviour.
- Pamper yourself by adopting positive methods: yoga, beauty care, dress care.
- De-stress yourself by seeking areas of your healthy interest which may keep you mentally and physically fit:
- Write down your problems or thoughts on paper in detail; it does not matter how terrible they are. Then tear and throw the paper away.
- Involve yourself in some light activities, preferably productive (e.g., sports, crafts, writing, music, painting, cooking etc.). Creative writing, painting, singing, dancing etc., not only provide an outlet

to your suppressed feelings but they can also give you a sense of liberation from your normal stressful routine. Some of the greatest authors, poets, painters, singers, dancers around the world have successfully converted their negative emotions into works of art. If you have a different method of reducing your anxiety, pursue it, like exercise, yoga, gardening etc.

Share your problems with like-minded people.

The best way to fine-tune your parental skill is to spend quality time with your own kids. Be an involved participant in their activities. Not only will this reduce your anxiety, but it will also encourage greater communication with your children. Frequent interaction with children is extremely important. Quality time includes playing, discussing, watching TV, sharing events etc., depending upon the age group of your child.

By adopting these methods, you will find a remarkable change in yourself, and your anxiety level will be reduced to a great extent. So you can handle anxiety in different ways. Adopt any of the aforesaid methods that appeals to you.

If you can control or find a way to reduce your anxiety, you will prove to be a competent parent; moreover, you can understand your child's stress better and help him cope with his own anxieties.

Conclusion:-

If parents were only a little less casual in advertising the dark edges of their personality to their children, we would surely have had a society of smarter, less erratic, fundamentally stronger (morally and psychologically) youth. Not only would they have been more in control of themselves but also possibly have steered clear of any behavioural aberration and prevented themselves from becoming the deviant from the accepted norms of the society.

INDISCIPLINE

Indiscipline covers a vast area of one's own habitual weaknesses and irregular activities (sleeping, eating, working hours, habit of using profane language, lack of courtesy, to name a few instances). In an extreme form, it encompasses addictions (alcohol, tobacco, and drug/substance abuse) and criminal activities (gambling, betting, cheating, lying, sexual-crime and fraud). These habits are entirely learnt and acquired, and largely relate to a person's surroundings, training, parental influence, peer-influence and mental make-up. However, if genetic influence is prominent, it adds fuel to fire.

It is usually seen that a person who has some bad habits is often prone to develop his intimacy with people of the same inclinations. How he talks, behaves and interacts with members of the society determine his parenthood-image. However, it is said that 'old habits die hard', which is true to some extent. But with the rapid changes in society today in every perspective, the old theories are also changing. So, sticking to the old methods may be instrumental in increasing confusion and conflicts in the parents of the modern age. No one is perfect in this world. Would-be parents who find themselves undisciplined in many ways should bring lots of changes in themselves prior to the arrival of their child. One is not supposed to stick to one's bad habits forever. A parent should have a clear idea of their own bad habits so that they can bring some changes in their sense of discipline. It needs positive efforts which come through a person's determination and strong will-power.

These days, parents are entirely unaware of how their own habits, internet and cellphone addictions, involvement in kitty parties, shopping mania and making extra money by indulging in immoral and fraudulent activities, create in children the feelings of rejection and negligence. As a sequel to all this, their children create their own self-involved world and exert their energy in wrong ways and dissipated their youth. The following cases relating to children show how parents' lack of discipline becomes detrimental to their own children's interests. The kids of such parents often become influenced by the wrong persons, who are usually much older to the kids.

Paresh, a twelve year old boy, had lots of complaints against his father. He was ashamed of his father's habit of using profane language. Moreover, both his parents were addicted to tobacco. His mother also had an extremely bad temper. The child used to feel lonely and often felt embarrassed and humiliated due to his father's unpredictable outbursts and uttering profane language. He was unable to find anybody with whom he could share his inner-most feelings. Consequently, he developed an intimacy with his care-taker, who used to be involved with the household work. He started smoking in his company, as this habit would induce within him a feeling of wellness.

Shivam, a ten year old boy, was very lazy because his parents had an unhealthy schedule. The reason behind his poor attention and restlessness was his irregularity in every activity, from taking a bath to sleeping. He was a late riser due to which he had to sacrifice most of the morning rituals. His mother could not figure out the reasons behind his recklessness towards his duties. Frequently, he used to leave for his school without performing his morning ablutions. The reason was that he had no time for even the necessary rituals, due to his lazy schedule. The parents had no clue how to reason with their child and explain to him the importance of punctuality, because they themselves lacked this trait completely. It is a well known maxim that nobody can pass on to another what he/she (parent in this case) himself/herself possessed. Since the parents themselves had no practice of adhering to punctuality, they completely failed to teach their child. Thus, the child was unable develop a sense of responsibility.

Fifteen year old, Shama, felt extremely displeased and rejected when she found her mother glued to the internet to make a lot of online male friends. Her mom often ignored Shama's emotional needs and desires. She had been brought to me for counselling because all of a sudden she had lost interest in her studies and had started spending all her time on the mobile. She was very hesitant to tell her mother about her embarrassment and distress. Hence, she started developing insecurities, fears, and loneliness, and was unable to cope with the fact that her mother was sharing her daughter's time with somebody else. Her mother's rejection was taking a toll on her studies and her mother was completely unaware of this fact.

Sixteen year old Ranbir could not relate himself to either of his parents.

"I do not know why my mom is always stuck to the computer. I think she has been playing some online betting games, and is involved in some sort of gambling?"

Ranbir's guess was true, because he had the same bent of mind. However, his mother was so addicted to gambling that she could not stop herself, and eventually ended up involving her son in the same games.

"On the other hand, my father often sticks to his cell phone. I guess he gives priority to his mobile rather than me."

His parents finally woke up from their stupor when Ranbir lost a lot of money while gambling with his friends. He started stealing jewellery and precious items from his home. Her mother said, "I was only doing this for the sheer entertainment. I could not comprehend that involving him in this pastime would lead him to such ends"

So the mother's excitement-seeking behaviour and child's addiction and gambling put them in an extremely dangerous situation.

There was another case involving an easy-going couple, who would frequent kitty parties. They would leave their eight-year-old son, Vishal, to the confines of their dwelling, in order to attend various social events. Of course, life came easy to Vishal since he possessed all the things that money could buy. But he missed the energy and the capacity to strive for doing better. Moreover, having lived in a house, rather than a home, throughout his childhood, he could not identify with feelings and affection. The parents surely cut a sorry figure, as they were completely unaware of this missing link in the child's rearing.

As years went by, the boy's parents' continued to neglect him and allowed him the chance to become extremely irresponsible and irrational, to such an extent that, by the time he turned thirteen, he had completely turned his back on school. That is when his parents understood the gravity of the situation. Visibly stunned, they came to me for help, having received a notice from their son's school, informing them of the child's truant behaviour.

The problems faced by the family cited above are fairly common, to say the least. According to the parents, they have behaved perfectly and have always been very cooperative. But they appeared, according to my reading, to have truly faltered by totally ignoring the daily needs of their children: Shama, Vishal and Ranbir. Without the element of supervision, their children had turned truant and had developed the sore feeling of neglect. The parents could not gather how their own personalities were influencing the child to develop the aforesaid traits.

Have you ever noticed that your lack of discipline puts your child at the risk of developing a host of problems? This is the worst kind of weakness in your personality. This may turn a child towards detrimental tendencies like addiction to drugs and alcohol, sexual aberrations and other signs of waywardness.

A child's indiscipline usually reflects the parents' own enjoyment-seeking behaviour which makes them blissfully unaware of the child's mental needs. Left to fend for himself, he gradually nurtures negative friendships. His uncontrolled wish to see his desires fulfilled, make him play truant from school. He might start preferring to keep unhealthy company, rather than attend school. Thus, a child with a tenuous attachment towards his parents, perhaps, develops a negative internal model of them, which eventually gives rise to hostility and truant behaviour in him.

"I grew up under the supervision of a caretaker. My parents' wealth never attracted me. I wished to have a normal family, like Minakshee's. I like Minakshee who is my neighbour and her family because she has a beautiful family. They take care of my needs and requirements." Prahalad, the son of one of a renowned and moneyed man, announced it very confidently. His parents were disapproving of his friendship with the girl and her family whose status was below average from their point of view.

Nikhil, a seventeen-year-old boy, who belonged to the higher strata of society, lost some lakhs of rupees in gambling and at that time his parents got a big shock. Nikhil showed acrimony towards his parents: "I was just following their instructions. They used to motivate me to mingle with the friends and join the club. I did exactly what they said. So I started mingling with my peer group there. What's the big deal if I lost money? I may get back the money by playing further. Now they are watching and objecting to my every movement.

A father was sitting before me and was disturbed with the habit of his thirteen year old daughter, Nandita. She craved for everything expensive and branded. It was her obsession. While complaining about his daughter's bad habits, the topic of conversation took a different turn, and all of a sudden Nandita's father confided in me: "See my cell phone. You know I'm almost the first buyer when a new mobile is launched in the city. This is my passion."

Where the parents are wrong?

A mother, Anamika, 35 years old, came to me for her six- year-old child, Arjun, due to his lying, excessive talkativeness, disobedience and stubbornness. I was myself dumbfounded when after delicate and thorough investigations I found that the parents of Arjun were both involved in several fraud cases. On his mother's part, her superficial charm, which is one of the prominent features of antisocial personality disorder, was the main tool to attract people and manipulate them accordingly. I further found that the mother was herself a compulsive liar and an unemotional and callous person. Her main asset to cheat people was her superficiality in every respect. But when her child adopted the same personality she was not able to see herself in the mirror. However, mothers with similar characteristics are found in large numbers. In such activities, sometimes the pairs work together. Husbands encourage their wives to utilize their charms and trap influential people, in order to achieve their targets.

The problem with such mothers is that they want to make easy and quick money. Parents who belong to this category have a problem in accepting their own shortcomings. Their rigidity becomes so much a part and parcel of their personalities that they often rationalize and justify their actions. The counselling of such parents are most of the time ineffective. Anamika was worried about her son, not about herself. She was putting forward lots of instances and convincing me that her actions were justified.

While adopting such methods, mothers should be careful of the repercussion of the artificiality of their behaviour (and, at the same time, making it a justifiable act) on their children. This trend is not related to their conflicting situations but to their habit of manipulation and manoeuvring.

"Children are an integral part of their parents; as long as the mirror is unclean, how can you expect the image to be pure?"

Enjoying kitty party, shopping and visiting spa or beauty parlour indicate your positivity and exuberance.

However, over-indulging in such activities shows your inability to cope with your personal situation and thus allowing problems to get accentuated.

It leaves an indelible impression on your child's psyche that you are escaping from your responsibilities and giving much importance to your own entertainment and recreation.

Parents! Listen carefully!

Your child is unable to cope with your continued absence, either physically or psychologically. If you are too busy with your own problems to listen to your child, you, as the parent, often fail to give your child the much-needed support during periods of crisis. This creates an emotional stress on the child and thereby paring the way for keeping distance between the parent and the child. Parents, you should not overlook the need to spend quality time with your children.

DISCIPLINING YOURSELF:

Never preach what you cannot practice.

- Do not force your child to study while you are partying or watching television in the next room.
- Do not force your child to sleep or eat according to your convenience.
- Do not lie to your child while you're leaving home to attend a party or going to a movie.
- Do not insult or scold your child in front of other members of your family or guests.
- The characteristics of your friends' circle have a big impact on your child. Be selective when it comes to choosing your friends.
- Make a routine for yourself and let your child follow it along with you.
- Respect your own elders before you expect your child to respect you.
- If you are habituated in passing indecent remarks about others, you end up setting a poor example for your child. Stop it immediately. Mind your language.
- If you are extravagant, be careful, for your child will imitate you.

So, parents! Don't behave in ways which you would not like your child to imitate.

In the words of J. Edgar Hoover (long-time Director of the FBI in the US):

'If discipline is practised in every home, juvenile delinquency would be reduced by 95%.'

Parents! Wake up!

Your child's attachment to you may be jeopardized when you fail to provide him with a warm, trusting, dependable and firm relationship.

What does your child want to see in you?

Warmth, dependability, trust, frankness, sincerity, concern for others, compliance and humility. Parents who lack these traits shatter the child's expectations.

Realisation and empathy are two essential feelings that work as a lighthouse showing you the right path, making you more mature, giving you more strength, and finally guiding you to adopt the right method while you are interacting with your kid as well as your spouse.

❑❑❑

Reminiscences

- *Parent as a Child*

Parent As A Child

I have found that a large proportion of the parents who come forward with various behavioural problems of their children have themselves been the victims of poor parenting and a disorderly home environment. These parents often start by complaining about their child's misdeeds or misbehaviour and end up narrating their own childhood traumas related to rejection, negligence by their parents, parental discord, financial problems, and poor home environment.

Parents' own socialisation and their interactions with their environment during childhood determine and predict their behaviour and actions. Parents who were the victims of bad parenting often suffer from lack of social and problem-solving skills, self-control, and difficulty in emotional reciprocation. Only those parents who identify the weaknesses of their own personality, which they have inherited from their parents, and start shaping them in a meaningful way, will be successful in being free of all those biases which they have retained for a long period of time.

In fact, parents' traits are deeply ingrained and the rigidity of their temperament often stops them from reconsidering and evaluating the demands of a particular situation. It is very much evident in their inability to meet the requirements of most situations.

Times, they are a rapidly changing phenomenon and so are we.

Analysing oneself in a rational way is the key mantra for success, especially when parenting issues are concerned.

The best way to keep yourself mentally fit is to accept the faults or ignorance of your parents, who unknowingly passed on their undesirable traits to you. Now you can correct yourself by developing an insight: NEVER REPEAT THEIR MISTAKES.

Now the suggestion for parents is **Look Back.**

So! Parents looking back sometimes give you an opportunity to filter out the dirt which you gathered during your childhood days. It makes you more vigilant and consistent while dealing with your child.

LOOK BACK!

Assess childhood deprivations: judge rationally.

Indulge in nostalgia for a moment.

More than two decades back you were a kid, an innocent kid who was completely unaware of the consequences of your naughtiness. Your parents were tired of your mischievous actions but you were still the apple of their eye.

Let us see how today's parents are comparing their own childhood deprivation and how they try to change their own style of parenting, but still not getting the desired result.

'...My father's financial limitations did not allow me to grow up in a proper way. In fact, living in a joint family, my father's priority was to take care of his brothers and their children. He used to avoid or neglect my demands. As a sequel to this, I suppressed many desires and even developed a kind of rivalry with my cousins who were better off than me now.

...My parents were worried about the condition of the family and they were looking forward to settling me in some job so that I could provide some financial security for them. I was trying to keep up my studies so that I could make a bright future for myself and earn more money to make my family happy and satisfied. Now I have everything... I'm trying to provide my child as much as I can and yet he has a lot of complaints against me. I'm at a loss as to why this is happening.'

'...It is very unfortunate situation that I used to watch a lot of quarrels between my parents related to financial, familial, and other personal problems, which kept me awake at night. Consequently, I hardly used to pay attention to my studies. I was too young to convey to them how severely I was getting affected by their discord. It was not an easy job for me to keep myself calm and controlled. Thus, I used to feel rejected and neglected by my own parents. But later on, when I became a parent, I decided that I will not let my child get affected by my personal and financial problems. I take care of my child in the best way I can... still he is not up to my expectations. I don't understand why.'

'...I'm the victim of poor parenting. My father was an alcoholic. I used to watch my mother's agony. In fact, she was herself a victim of my father's temper and tantrums. Her depression and father's alcoholism taught me many things. I don't drink. I know the trauma of a child with disturbed parents. My first priority is my child and I want to provide him with good parenting. But I observe that still he is indifferent towards me. I'm in a dilemma. Why does he behave the way he does?'

' ....My parents had set some strict rules. My siblings and I were supposed to obey the rules without raising any objection. Now it's my turn to maintain the family rules and regulations and I don't want to destroy the peace so I relaxed and liberated them from such restrictions. Still my child is not happy. He often keeps quite and withdrawal. We tried to comprehend his problems but in vain. We are worried: why does he act like this?'

WHY?

Parents have many complaints against their children, in spite of their personal effort in supervising them. I observed that the parents' way of supervision was perceived in their own light. They were convinced that there was no problem with their own way of parenting. To some extent they were correct. But what they could not figure out was that the manner in which their children perceived their parents' parenting style also plays a crucial role while dealing with them. So, in order to prove themselves as competent, it is essential for the parents to see themselves through their child's eyes, which certainly their own parents could have missed.

The child's perception of his parents' behaviour should be taken into consideration when one evaluates his parenting. Then parents will be able to discover the missing factors which their child perceives quite clearly. So the crux of the problem lies in the disparity of the perceptions between the two: the Parent and the Child.

The following statements may provide some insights into the thinking of the parents while assessing/visualizing their own deprivations in childhood.

During a group session of parents on "Parents' own Parenting: An Analytical Approach", I flung a question before them:

'Do you feel that you were not loved by your parents?'

'I'm afraid, it's true. Since they were my parents, they did love me but their rules and regulations were so strict, I never felt affection from their side.'

It is a common affirmation from many parents.

'Could you ever detect any hidden affection in your parents for you?'

'It would be very sad for me to deny it! But no! I didn't!'

I wanted to be very clear on their perception about their parents.

'Do you think that your parents really had no affection for you?'

'Oh! No!... it's not exactly that...but something was missing in their mode of parenting...can't exactly put it in words. Sometimes they were very careless and sometimes very strict so it's really difficult to figure out.' Hence, indeed the situation is inexplicable.

The parents were confused and hesitant at this juncture.

This confusions and inability to perceive affection on the part of their parents only goes to show that parents are ignorant about the importance of expression of love in words, gestures and hugs which are readily perceived by their child. They usually are very careless about the relationship with their child. They regard their child as their personal commodity and end up often toying with their feelings inadvertently. Their lack of awareness and insufficient knowledge about the delicate nature of this relationship deprive them of an understanding of the value and weight of the expressions of love and affection. Ultimately, they have to pay the price for their ignorance by making their own child confused, restless, and anxious, and an insecure human being.

Present-day parents, in fact, are overcoming those obstacles which they met during their own childhood. They are habituated to pin-pointing the deprivations during their childhood. Comparing the missing factors during their own time and the present makes them confused because they fail to realise that the needs of a child have increased manifold in the interim period and, above all, they could not replace the 'missing factor' (i.e., child's perception of love and affection) which is entirely an abstract need, intangible.

Affection needs to be expressed in words, gestures and touch, especially while you interact with your family, because you are the most significant person in your child's life. Expression of love is as important as the food one eats or the water one drinks, without which one cannot even imagine surviving. It is one of the vital needs which are biologically oriented. The perception of being loved, in terms of hugging, kissing, patting, encouraging and other soft forms of show of emotion, is the first emotional need of a child. Moreover, it shows your affectionate communication skill which is the only way to send the message of the heart. To reiterate, expression of love is the elixir of life.

Dear Parents! You must learn to express it!

Thus the child's perception of his parents' love and affection seems to be a vital factor to be reckoned with, while parents tend to execute positive parenting, but do not get positive feedback from their child.

Hang on! Take a few minutes and recall that when you hugged your child last time?

When you expressed how much you love him? Did you make your habit to highlight his good deeds by saying, Nice, Wonderful, and Carry on dear?

GENETIC INFLUENCE

It is true that behavioural problems are most likely to arise when genetically vulnerable children are not treated in a healthy way. In such cases, the only way to tackle the problems is being a responsible and sincere parent. There are several parents who have mild to severe inclination towards alcohol, betting, gambling and other detrimental habits or addictions. Some of them try to control these aberrations but not completely. Their children may have a strong mental inclination towards alcohol and gambling.

Dear Parents! you should know the formula of controlling your child's lust and desires. First and foremost, you need to know the causes of your problems. If it is genetic do not blame your parents. Because you will be wasting your time if you maintain the same addictions and disorders. The best way to reduce these problems across generations is to attempt to reduce your own genetically-oriented negative traits. This reduction may be helpful for the next generation and the problems may subside by degrees.

Today's parents are much more aware of, and concerned about, the psychological and physical welfare of their child, and are ready to modify their own undesirable traits for the betterment of their child's psyche.

They understand the importance of parenting and are also inclined to bring about certain changes in their inherited negative traits to stop the trend of recycling of particular forms of behaviour. It is widely known that the combination of genetic vulnerability and poor parenting leads to an aggravation of behavioural problems in a child.

Shipra and Saket had shared their problems with me. Their eleven-year-old child was paying more attention to the share market than to his studies. They were both quite surprised and sad at how their little kid was so influenced by this habit at such a tender age. Their case further went on to reveal that the child's paternal grandfather was a gambler and had lost all his money in the share market and in gambling. Saket was depressed because he had worked hard for his family, yet he would still keep a keen eye on the happenings of the share market, even though he was not at all addicted to it.

He opened up to me: "Yes, I can't deny it. I have a very sharp knowledge about the share market; however, I have lost all interest due to my father's carelessness and destructive tendencies. I was never able to forgive my father for his conspicuous lapses, and so I decided that I will not involve myself in this dirty and ruinous game. As a matter of fact, I do have a little inclination towards the share market but I'm far too hard-headed and tough-minded to let any addiction get the better of me. My only motivation is to work towards establishing my child's career."

He accepted that he keeps track of the share market through newspapers and television, but he had never dreamed that his son would fall prey to this addiction. There are several parents such as Saket, who do not realise that their children can be easily influenced by their genetic traits from a very tender age.

There is a piece of advice which I gave to Saket:

'First of all, check your own worries. Then start discussing with your child on different aspects, ranging from sports to the share market. Do not highlight the share market as the main topic, but keep talking about movies, music and other light things related to your child's interests. When you find that your child is comfortably placed with you, he will voluntarily start talking to you about his habits and inclinations. You have to realise that when you forbid him something or preach against something excessively, your child's curiosity and adamantine characteristics will be aroused, and it has the opposite effect and your son may develop further interest in those things. You should discuss with your son at length about the crises your father faced due to the share market, and how you had to work past that to reach where you are now. Relating to your child on a personal level and being open and honest with him about your own apprehensions will establish a clear and open line of communication between the two of you; and this will develop a strong, trusting and lasting relationship. On the other hand, in such cases, openly criticising the grandparents will only aggravate your problem. You have to be extremely careful to avoid either extreme. Be sensitive to the issue without being over-critical, and you will do both yourself and your child a lot of good.'

YOUR TEMPERAMENT

Parents who were brought up in poor or disturbed home environments or dysfunctional families show either impulsiveness or depression in their temperament while dealing with their child's problems and issues.

The parents who belong to this category are less likely to learn the appropriate skills required for effective social adaptation. Their own childhood experiences and inability to contend with the situations largely affect their feeling of well-being, which is directly linked to their interactions with their child.

Thus, one's own parental actions and behaviour, unwittingly and constantly, have a profound influence on the child, and it becomes visible only when people around them start whispering, 'Like father like son…'. 'chip of the block'.

It is advisable for parents, to find out the flaws in their parents' parenting and based on that adopt new methods to avoid an emotional break-up with their child. Visualising your parents' improper attitude may provide some vital clues on 'how to impart good parenting' to your own children. It is unfortunate that most parents refuse to accept their own weaknesses because their ingrained traits become so much a part of their personality that they no longer seem a matter of concern. with the result, they cannot perceive how that might have any adverse impact on their children.

There are many factors that might have affected you or influenced your behaviour. As a result, you often try to trace the reasons for your present anxiety, depression, rigidity and anger, and defend yourself by blaming or accusing your parents' negligence and carelessness, either directly or indirectly.

Parents, identify your problem areas and work towards them. Because parenting is not an innate trait but an acquired skill which one can only learn through experience either own experience or others experience by being more thoughtful and rational. In an alcoholic/ criminal family (where the father is affected), a child does not learn the values of the family because of the stress produced by the father. This is why he hardly knows how to interact sensibly and how to be an important member and be involved as a part of the family. The child becomes deficient in feelings of sharing and caring. Sometimes he keeps himself emotionally detached from the members of the family, or he becomes oversensitive and reacts to every insignificant issue. Moreover, he may develop a social anxiety which prevents him from establishing good communications with the people around him. A good mother can stand as a buffer and nurture her child in the right manner. But utmost care must be exercised to ensure that the buffer strength is invariably maintained, in order to avert any conflict between the parents inter se. There are several such kinds of examples where mothers stand as the pillars of strength for their kids. To remove your fears associated with your own childhood experiences, you may try the following method:

Tranquilizing Effect

Parents! To keep yourself fresh, it is better to select the good memories, separating them from the chain of bad memories of your childhood. Some people have a natural tendency to do that, filtering out the latter, and so they are less likely to be adversely affected by their own experiences in childhood while dealing with their child's problems. They find a smooth way to sail quietly even in the stormy seas of life, overcoming their own childhood stress and trauma.

But parents who are often preoccupied with their own painful past tend to behave in a completely different way: being aggressive, depressive, authoritarian or inconsistent. They are prone to blame their own chaotic backgrounds and end up overlooking the present demands of their child.

Everybody has a soft corner in their heart filled with certain good memories. The problem lies in the parents' habit of highlighting only the sad memories of their childhood and wallowing in their grey experiences. As a result, they often dwell on the dark days, and this gets reflected in their negative lifestyle. They are so confused and obsessed regarding their childhood experiences that they find it difficult to adjust to the present. If a person tries to pick the good memories from the plethora of traumatic ones, it will certainly enhance their self-confidence and motivate them to move in a positive direction. Parents! If you dwell overlong in your childhood's unhappy memories, you cannot sort out your child's problems.

I give below in a nutshell a list of complaints and grievances which the parents faced in their childhood:

- Parental discord or adjustment-problem: may be due to disagreement over minor issues;
- Large family: resulting in neglect of children;
- Parents' ignorance and lack of awareness;
- Fathers' inclination towards the outer world, (spending time with the friends and the persons of their choice only;
- Fathers' lower degree of involvement in family matters, related to studies and standard of living;
- Father an alcoholic/gambler with a criminal background;
- Financial setback;

- Parents' angry temperament—reflected in yelling, hitting and spanking, mothers' indifferent attitude towards the kids;
- Parental bias towards particular child resulting in sibling rivalries.

What is astonishing behind the above complaints is that present-day parents speak of their progressiveness and changed behaviour vis-à-vis their parents but the root cause of the problems remains unchanged.

I have a list of complaints of today's parents in a more advanced form. With the efflux of time, their grievances have assumed more sophisticated patterns. However, the nature of problems remain basically the same with dimensional variations.

The following complaints are expressions of the primary problems they face with their child:

'I feel helpless and get restless when I see the report card of my son.'

'My son's friends are spoiling him. I am frustrated as I find him very stubborn and disobedient. I guess he has taken to smoking and drinking.'

'My daughter is blindly following the modern trend. She has a large number of male friends. I despise it; I always live in a state of fear and anxiety. She is very obstinate. When I tell her anything she either immediately leaves the room or shouts at me.'

'I am scared of my son's rash driving. He often leaves home without informing me. Most of the time he has his lunch and dinner outside.'

'My daughter is creating lots of problems. She does not want to stay with us. She is hunting for a paying guest accommodation to leave us and be independent. She is just sixteen.'

"My son often stays aloof. He does not share any of his feelings with us. He prefers to be alone. He has no friends. Either he watches television or he studies. He does not enjoy any social or personal gatherings. I am very much worried about him.'

'My son's demands are increasing by leaps and bounds. It's scary because they are often expensive…ranging from a costly cell phone to an expensive car…"

What I have concluded is that most of the parents have grievances against their children and either hold a rigid family rule or remain indifferent. As a result, they are either strict or lax which reduces their competence as parents. Most of them revealed own childhood experiences including parental domination, strict family rules or aloofness, indifference, apathy and/or depression. When parents show their difficult temperament by having negative responses towards their child that certainly is going to jeopardize the pleasing ambience of the home situation.

If parents find that they are governed by their inherited bad traits they should try to reform themselves as soon as possible.

Moderation and discipline are keywords for the best teaching. Today a society with high demands where parents focus on the limited issues of their child's needs which are only approved by them is creating a dilemma in their child about what to do and what not to do.

Parents generally overlook what they themselves do: how they are often anxious to compete with their colleagues, friends and relatives in every aspect of life by hook or by crook. If they find themselves relatively unsuccessful they start dreading the outcome. As a result, they become victims of their own frustrations. Their frustrations have a profound impact on their child, for they become more irritable and aggressive. It is the primary duty of parents to brush aside their own issues which block the way to simplicity, goodness, a progressive outlook and humanity.

COMPARISON AND COMPENSATION: UNHEALTHY MODES

The parents' own complexes, insecurity and deep-rooted anxiety which cast a shadow on their child-rearing practice may be detrimental to the child.

These parents are helpless and indecisive most of the time. Occasionally, they are liable to impart a sort of parenting which tends to compensate for their own complexes and they end up providing the things which they were denied in their youth without considering the consequences. If not directly or intentionally, this may have some link with the parents' deep-rooted unfulfilled desires which they want to gratify by regimenting or spoiling the child. Parents should be careful about not going to either extreme.

Another set of parents move in a direction opposite to this trend. They feel that the child should be treated in exactly the same way as they were treated in their childhood, recalling their parents as harsh, conservative and non-rewarding. They become inconsiderate or follow blindly their self-made or customary rules and compel their child to obey the same. This rigidity is hardly accepted by their child. Very soon he turns a deaf ear and starts revolting against their commands, orders and even requests. Parents' constant refusals to demands may make a child more stubborn and take him far away from his parents.

I have observed during interview sessions that many parents forced their child to follow the rules which they have been observing for generations. Although it is not bad to maintain the family rituals, to follow each and every rule without modification and mutual agreement, in conformity with the needs of the changing times, the idea sounds like autocracy. Many children are the victims of their parents' autocratic nature. Sometimes, parents' adamant attitude is the by-product of their learnt behaviour which they take as normal, as it is the training they received in their own childhood. Whatever they learnt then, they consider an absolutely normal way of behaving.

Discover Good Options

Approximately, two decades back, society was quite different. There have been lots of changes since then; how can you stop your child from going along with the new trend? Rather, you need to bring some progressive changes in yourself and your behaviour without needlessly comparing the modern times to the olden days. You can overturn the notion that one's personality and disposition cannot be changed. You are quite capable of originating a new principle on your own by bringing a positive change in your attitude and outlook.

Thus, for parents, compensating for their own deprivations or insistence upon adhering to the old family practice of child-rearing is, in either case, based on their biases. There is no plausible reason why parents should not respond to the novelty and the changes which are happening rapidly around them. The child who accepts rigid parental dictates may develop an inflexible and restricted personality and face guilt-arousing and self-abasing conflicts, resulting in mounting and severe problems in them. So, you should be a liberal parent—while proceeding carefully!

Parents! It is advisable for you to sort out your position by reviewing your parental problems at periodic intervals and their traumatic impact on you which block the way to your becoming more liberal and independent. It will open new vistas for you to welcome new and good ideas, thereby enabling you to develop a correct insight, and realize the severity of the actions of your own troubled past and their ongoing impact on your child.

Parents will find some illustrations in the following chapter on how their own behaviour crosses over to their child willy nilly. It is good idea for them if they assess themselves by relegating themselves to the background as a 'child' inside them and interact with 'him' accordingly.

There are so many families who demonstrate how even a person who came from a disturbed family raises his child in the right direction. So one's own childhood experiences may give one some vital clues on what to do and what not to do— let those guide one's activity.

Ragini, a mother of two teenage children, said "I used to see many fights between my parents from my very early childhood. Dad used to torture my mom. My mom was often in depression. She hardly supervised us, as I have a brother, too. We both used to take care of ourselves. We used to manage from school to home by ourselves. We were deprived of many essential childhood desires. Now, my husband and I share a wonderful relationship and we're bonding with our kids. We are satisfied with our achievements. We celebrate every occasion with zest. We often drop in on our relatives and friends. We don't spend much time with friends, rather we make sure that we give our children maximum time. Both my children are excellent. I don't find that my traumatic childhood experience interfered with my own life. Rather, it enriched my over all experience which gave me some insight and taught me the secret of family happiness which we often lacked."

In the final analysis, a parent blaming a child for some behavioural disorders needs to look back to his early days of parenting and find hints for a correct approach in his personal history.

Personality traits and the quality of the marriage are interdependent. Both pinpoint to how you will mould your child. A child's behaviour is the reflection of the parent's own image. A marriage needs lots of discipline.

❑❑❑

PART-II

Lust or Creation?

- *Flaws in one's married life which affect a child's entire life*
- *Solution with lots of tips*

Marital Discord – Traumatic for Child

Marriage is one of life's most significant, and in many ways, difficult responsibilities. It has, and makes, its own demands. A spouse, when unable to cope with the stresses of his/her marital life, develops unhealthy habits and qualities, which has far-reaching consequences for everyone involved.

Kaka's father threw away his plateful of meal and shouted, "Who is forcing you to cook? If you can not cook then why are you wasting my money on such kind of food? … Don't you know this is my place."

Kaka's mother was no less harsh, "all your things are lying here and there. Can't you use your wardrobe?"

"What the hell is a wardrobe? I'll keep all my clothes on the bed; what will you do?" His father yelled and dragged all of his ironed clothes and other stuff from the wardrobe and flung them on the floor, cursing, "You…!"

His mother screamed, "Hey! Mind your language...!"

This is what I was compelled to listen to at Kaka's home while playing some indoor game. Ultimately, we stopped going to his home. Kaka had to snuff out his keen desire to entertain his friends at home. Frankly speaking, this chain of events became a nightmarish experience for me.

Times have certainly changed today. Interactions between couples have taken a different turn now, even though the fundamental dissimilarities remain the same. Quarrels have started taking new and different directions, assuming serious proportions. These days, in the age of fast-track conversations and time-bound interactions, as the factors of communication between spouses become even more limited, couples seem to have very little faith left in each other. Often, both spouses work, and consequently, develop separate groups of friends, and by acting upon, in consonance with the so called well-wisher's advice, the affected parents end up lacking in common interests and reasons for happiness and enjoyment. Due to this absence of common grounds to bind them together, they slowly start drifting apart, and in worst-case scenarios, this can ultimately lead to a complete breakdown of communication which further undermines the very foundations of marriage. This trend is now growing rapidly in the Indian set-up. Couples who disregard the basic premises of the institution of marriage, unfortunately, end up losing respect for their other halves, and this situation is further complicated when they have kids. Even at a very early stage of such distancing and disagreements, their kids' mindset and psyche are very deeply affected. In such cases, parents begin to find out very soon that their child is turning hostile towards them and the consequences are almost always the same as those in Kaka's case.

A Few Words For Parents!

Giving birth to a child is one of the most beautiful aspects of a couple's life. As a parent, you are rendering your most valuable creation to the society. You can hold your head high now because you feel that you have added a good civilian to the population. But you will have done your bit only after reaching your goal of nurturing your child in the right manner. This frees you from other challenging issues in your life such as old-age worries. Now you are more competent and capable of acquiring enough strength to go ahead and face the newer challenges in life.

No matter how much money you earn, and fame you garner, your conscience will always mark you down as a 'failure' if you are unable to provide your child a good upbringing through continuous projection of your own problems relating to interpersonal relationships within your family.

If these personal problems get accentuated to such an extent as capable of overpowering you, you will only end up detaching yourself from the quite wonderful possibilities of family bonding and togetherness. As this situation unfolds itself, in the ultimate analysis, your child will be unable to perceive you in a positive light, because, as you fight restlessly inside the shell of your own issues, your focus and priority shifts away from your family, very much to your discomfiture. Eventually, it is your child who becomes the victim of your frustrations, for the simple reason that you become so prone to giving vent to your inner turmoil by throwing a tantrum against your own creation that you ultimately keep distancing yourself and losing the vital emotional connection that you share with your child.

A child, unable to fight back against his parents' indifferent or harsh attitude, begins to find himself helpless. Bitter, acrimonious arguments between spouses (as in Kaka's case) may fill a child with aggressive, dangerous thoughts and this might lead him on to unforeseen, perilous paths. When this aggression reaches its climax, he needs and searches for an outlet to get rid of it and, more often than not, ends up manifesting it in harmful ways.

Just take five minutes to form a mental picture of your child's possible misdeeds: aggression, addiction, substance abuse, delinquency, depression, loneliness and withdrawal. Is this what you desire for him? Think about it.

Marriage Is Not A Herculean Task. You Have Accepted It Willingly and For A Valid Reason

Marriage is a long journey. You need to equip yourself with all the necessary qualities (psychological, physical and financial) to counter the trivial or non-trivial problems of your family and present yourself as a near-panacea for all the ills related to your spouse and kids. Adhere to the basic family principles. After all, you have taken a vow before God to take responsibility for your family and that is something which should never be taken lightly. Shirking your family responsibility and shrinking from your commitments constitute anathema to the will of God. Do not impede your child's growth by being too critical towards your spouse. Check your negative dispositions as soon as possible. Get prepared! Be careful! You are going to breed a new generation which is only recognized exclusively by your name, i. e., Mr or Mrs X /Y/ Z's generation.

A problem rarely crops up abruptly. It is a slow and gradual culmination of certain minor deviations and disagreements. However, one should remember that conflicts must be encountered in such a manner as they only makes the marriage stronger. Problems are not always your enemies: they make you realize your own fallible humanity and should, if treated correctly, make you realize the importance of the support and love of your partner. Small instances of strife should only work towards immunizing your family from other larger troubles. However, a large number of couples have lost their faith in the institution of marriage because they have neither the patience nor the courage to face the exacting demands of such situations. That is why many marriages are falling apart these days. Lamentably, most couples are so bent on making mountains out of molehills that they end up exhausting themselves and are too weak to stand their ground when the larger problems of life crop up. They are so engaged in fighting for their own rights that they seem to forget the psychological trauma that their kids must be going through. Couples' self-centredness and focus on their own enjoyment at the cost of interpersonal relationships are common reasons which disturb the healthy atmosphere of the home. They get carried away by greed, lust and desires and give priority to obtaining their own pleasure. These behavioural trends are quite threatening to healthy interpersonal relationships.

Marriage is a joint venture. It cannot be turned into a selfish endeavour. There has to be as much 'give' in marriage as there is 'take'; its success and strength depend on this delicate balance. When you add children into this complex equation, their well-being and happiness has to be made priority No.1. It is of decisive importance to remember that the sacrifices you make today are for a larger cause, a cause bigger than yourself, and having consequences more far-reaching than you can begin to imagine. Sometimes, you need to lose a battle, in order to win a war.

No Gender War Please

Gender bias exists. It is very much a truth. However, it is imperative that this should not disturb the harmony of a family. Men and women have certain distinct traits, characteristic reactions, differences in thoughts and actions. It is important for a couple to recognise these differences, work towards a compromise and to weave their disparate schools of thoughts into a single, synchronised fabric of a balanced family life.

Men and women are brought up with different ways of thinking. This becomes obvious within all their interactions, and is, in fact, essential for their conjugal life. As a concept, this is very healthy, as it keeps the sense of vitality, logic and balance alive in their judgements and responsibilities. However, if the balance starts shifting to either side, and instead of being complementary, it turns confrontational, it will also begin to affect the child adversely. Petty quarrels between spouses are not a matter of grave concern. In fact, they add value. Small arguments are inevitable in a relationship; they help in clearing the air, making your views known to your spouse, and keeping your mind fresh and uncluttered.

After all, two distinct individuals each belonging to different gender are brought together to live coherently under the institution of marriage are bound to have diversity of opinion; but neither of there should become opinionated. As the problems come, so, too, do the solutions. However, when these arguments become personal, and start being used as tools for vengeance and bitter insults, rather than opportunities to find solutions, then you begin to cross a dangerous line.

For a Husband

In the Indian set-up, when a woman marries her husband and comes to live in his family's house, she initially gets exposed to a "convention-shock". The social and family structure in her new settings might be completely different from the environment that she has been raised in, and her inability to come to terms with this new milieu, gives rise to this convention-shock. Here, it is of decisive importance for the husband to play a critical role and act with high sense of responsibility and a great deal of patience to resolve the conflicts and help her adjust in this entirely new, and somewhat alien, world. However, without offering any help in these difficult times, if the husband expects his wife to reconcile immediately the differences between her two separate ways of family life – one with her parents and the other (new) with her husband – it will lead to a degradation of their relationship and result in creating a chaotic family environment.

It may be generally true that often husbands have a pre-conceived nation that their wives are incompetent and intellectually inferior, and the latter's suggestions are often seen as irrelevant and thus ignored. It is in such prejudiced atmospheres that arguments scale up to extreme forms of violence e.g. domestic violence which merits criminal action against the guilty. Children, rarely having a say in these matters, end up as innocent victims of this adult apathy.

A family requires a head with a flexible personality, and this role traditionally belongs to a father, especially in the Asian family set-up. To be fair, men often have to encounter a different set of problems from their female counterparts, be it financial or otherwise. This does upset their composure, putting them under a lot of strain, and thereby often making them sacrifice psychological needs of greater significance. Again, this eventually establishes a permanent friction in their family life, emerging as it usually does even from petty differences. These problems get accentuated and assume alarming proportion over a period of time; gradually, leaving a profound impact on the offspring—a setback that remains throughout the life.

Husband's inflated egos, which keep them from losing ground, or expressing their vulnerabilities to their family, make them look out for a different set of people to vent their emotions on to satisfy their own needs. This new company of friends acts as a barrier to greater intimacy with the family, and again distances them from their children. This new, parallel life may not be accepted by your children, who require emotional closeness with their father to develop their own self-esteem and balanced perspectives.

It is natural and human for people to be a little rigid in their thoughts and perceptions. However, an excessive amount of this rigidity turns you into an authoritarian person, who cannot tolerate changes and will go to extreme lengths to prevent his viewpoint from being challenged. For most men, flexibility, sadly, means playing second fiddle to their wives, which is perceived as emasculating and demeaning. This bloated male ego is frequently a factor in situations and eventualities which end up ruining the atmosphere of a family.

Watching these ego-clashes and often one-sided arguments has a huge subconscious effect on children and leaves them helpless in their search for a resolution to the overbearing problems. The vulnerable child is now exposed to the risk of developing negative and confused views towards life—a direct consequence of his parents' conflicting tenets of life.

In patriarchal families, the male is the unquestionable head, with women being pushed to a weaker and inferior position. The father develops the habit of taking out all his angst and frustrations, built up inside him due to everyday anxieties, on his family. The stern tone of authority in his voice is ostensibly to create an aura of fear around him, and establish his dominance over the other members of the family. In such families, wives, annoyed by their husbands' inexorable and forceful nature, frequently begin sharing their misgivings with their increasingly fearful and oppressed children. Thus, the victims of the father's authoritarian traits create their own closed group, suitably cutting off the father's hegemony from it. The father, unable to comprehend this anomaly, ends up becoming even more frustrated, and the difference between the spouses continues to grow day by day, adding fuel to the fire. Ultimately, it is the fathers who become the sole sufferers of their own inflexibilities, often leaving their desperate family behind.

For a Wife

Through centuries of oppression and subjugation of women, there has been an attempt to subconsciously implant in the mind of women their physical and intellectual inferiority with respect to men. However, times have changed very rapidly, undoing a lot of the evil of the past centuries. In the modern age, an overwhelming majority of the female mindset has undergone a radical change, leading to an era of woman's independence and empowerment. Today, it is imperative for women to realise the importance of this intellectual liberty, and the pitfalls of falling into the age-old traps of male domination, which only serves to show women's inadequacies. Falling prey to this trap further devalues your existence and worth in your husband's eyes. This has to be avoided at all costs. Women mature earlier than men, and become even more dignified after marriage. As a woman, it is your right and, in fact, your responsibility to stand up for equality in terms of respect, opinions and values in your family. Your child especially wants and needs to see you as a free-thinking, independent individual. It strengthens his level of confidence and re-establishes his faith in the whole system of the family. However, as with everything in life, even the opposite extreme can be harmful. You have to be extremely cautious not to misuse this liberty. Your independence will always give you ample opportunities to exploit such situations to your benefit, by dealing with your child's problems without your husband's interference. However, be warned, this will have an extremely polarising effect on your family, and is as much an evil as is subservience. It is essential that both parents have an equal say in matters relating to the family, especially your children. You should discuss these issues with your spouse in a calm and dispassionate manner and any decision you take should be finally based on the consensus of both the parents. Remember, equality is for everyone!

A female's most common trait is to be nagging. She nags out of anxiety. She easily gets depressed. After childbirth, she becomes more concerned about her child than her husband. Husbands, generally, are unaware of this sensitive issue and may take it as a personal insult. Express it with a good grace. Babbling often creates a vacuum or brings a storm between the couples.

A large number of wives' woes relate to their husbands' indifferent attitude towards them due to their opacity.

When you discover the reason of his being not transparent you will be able to break the ice between the two of you. You will be a successful and happy partner if you equate/identify some of your husband's child-like characteristics wisely… A husband's tantrum should not be taken so seriously. Unfortunately, wives take it like a prestige-issue and become intolerant. Husband and wife start insulting and ignoring each other which may take a grim turn.

The Modern Spouse

Let me give you a brief introduction of how I perceived the modern marriage develop. The basic nature of the modern marriage is composed solely of superficial attraction, and knee-jerk reactions, without any forethought given to different compatibilities and complementary qualities. This kind of marriage essentially lacks a strong base for trust and respect, ab initio.

A majority of modern spouses seem to be immature and uncertain about the real meaning of marriage. Their marriage is initially based on imagination and fantasies, and when they finally realise the difficult truth of the non-existence of an 'effortless marriage', they often tend to shy away from putting in the requisite amount of work and inputs into it.

The different roles that a spouse has to enact are ever-changing, and very few people are willing to accept these changes. A marriage challenges you to find your own self within another person, search for happiness and satisfaction through the medium of a person other than yourself, throw away your rigidities and egoisms, and embrace the beauty of a perfect union. For a majority of people, marriage turns out to be so much greater and more formidable than they had imagined that they are immediately taken aback by the enormity of what they have undertaken. And, ultimately, they crack under pressure of this burgeoning weight and find it easier to give up than to fight on. This is precisely why we are seeing the rapid trend of divorce quickly following marriage. Unfortunately, parallel to this trend, there is another which makes the situation completely pathetic: having a child very quickly after marriage.

In today's world, women often earn as much, or even more, than their husbands. This might lead the husband to develop an inferiority complex, or conversely, the wife to develop a superiority complex; and either one of these can turn out to be extremely detrimental to the marriage. When handled improperly and immaturely, this unequal gap in the earning power, with the balance shifted in the woman's favour, seeps into the couple's personal lives as well, creating an emotional gap between them. It is imperative for the couple not to focus on this financial disparity, but, instead, pool in their money to create a common budget. The money should not be looked upon as belonging to a certain individual, but rather, as belonging to the whole family. This will result in greater harmony within the family and ensure a safe and secure future for the children as well. The husband's jealousy, inferiority complex, insecurities and rivalry, arising due to his counterpart's higher remuneration, better job status or a more successful professional life, should not get in the way and cause harm to their conjugal life.

Marriage is supposed to be an institution and your family occupies the entire space of its hallowed premises. It is reckless and immature to have children soon after marriage, even as your marriage has not yet been established on sound and resolute grounds. A child completely changes and disintegrates all equations. It turns your world upside-down, and brings about changes in your relationship with your spouse. If you have not put in enough time and effort into your marriage to form strong and stable bonds with your spouse, you will never be ready to survive the major upheavals that a child will most definitely cause. Unfortunately, couples, careless in 'love', and immature in thoughts, do not see this coming. What follows can be as devastating in a weak relationship as it is beautiful in a strong one.

Nevertheless, it should be distinctly understood that planning for a child even at the incipient stage of the couple's married life should be devised with the mutual consent of the couple themselves.

Generally speaking, the meaning of marriage is 'to create'. This creation in the form of their own baby brings heavenly pleasures for both the spouses. They love their children boundlessly. But their responsibilities increase with passing of time. Their natural care and affections for their spouse start shifting to their kid. The problems start right from here. Both the spouses start feeling neglected by his/her counterpart without a realization that life can change with the increased responsibilities and liabilities. These natural and real circumstances are bound to come. Their expression of love slowly turns into profane and acrimonious language. They start blaming each other for any meaningless reason. They find themselves neglected and rejected by their spouse. They feel great satisfaction in accusing their spouse for their kids' faults and misbehaviour. This is the other side of love which turns into hate and accusation just after the birth of their desired kid.

If only the married couples had realized that the child (or the newly born infant) is a trait of the parents and in the veins (including the pulmonary vein) of the infant child, the very parents blood is conveying, there should have been no occasion for the parents to quarrel on the grounds of treating the infant/child as separate.

Integrity In Diversity: Fusion of Distinct Interests, and Co-operation

A marriage requires adjustment and compromise, qualities integral for its sustainability. However, such change and self-sacrifice is a tough task for anyone, and not surprisingly so. Each partner in the marriage tries hard to keep his/her identity and perspectives intact, in the process of wishing the other half to live along the same lines. Obviously, this becomes far too much to expect, and due to the inflexibilities on either side, differences do remain in many aspects. Such long-festering differences of opinions and viewpoints ultimately take a turn for the worse, and when the dam finally breaks, a flood of unhappiness, discord and pain is released and the children's situation is analogous to that of the displaced persons or refugees—requiring rehabilitation immediately. Some couples try to work out a stop-gap solution to keep the tensions at bay, for the sake of their child, by refusing to communicate openly and resorting to external dependencies to fill the vacuum of love and support. This severely affects their marital life, and consequently, they go through emotional turmoil, which not only affects their own physical and psychological constitution, but also, often unintentionally, ends up hampering the healthy growth of their child.

A good marriage involves a well-balanced outlook and fulfilment of the wishes, desires, needs and duties of both the partners without any feelings of prejudice, jealousy or injustice. A successful marriage requires compromise and sacrifice, ensuring equal importance to the interests and wants of the spouses. When this balance becomes skewed in either direction, discord and disagreements start rearing their ugly heads.

The most important ingredient in the recipe of a successful marriage involves the successful, pleasant and balanced combination of desires and mutual respect for each other's interests and requirements. It also includes equal, unforced participation in activities and decisions made by the other partner and unconditional support to your spouse. Accept it as a normal phenomenon. Marriage in itself indicates a new beginning of your life. Never take it as liabilities. You are not sacrificing nor compromising. You are taking it as your integral part.

In a nutshell, conflicting personalities, with no attempt at reconciling these differences, drive spouses apart.

Look at some of the usual personality-differences which may form the root cause of marital discord:

- You are an introvert but your spouse being extrovert is outgoing.
- You are imaginative while your spouse is down-to-earth.
- You tend to be conservative while your spouse is liberal.
- You are authoritarian while your spouse is democratic. There is one or more of such different personality clashes.

Such distinct/opposite traits can have an adverse effect on the marriage, if the partners are unwilling to let go of their rigidities and compromise. These contrasting traits can lead to mal-adjustment, thus causing chaos and disturbances in interpersonal relationships. These insecurities and disagreements have a trickle-down effect which seeps into the child, playing havoc with his psychological and emotional development. Personality-differences are but natural, and are extremely difficult to accept and adapt. In all such situations, flexibility and adjustment capabilities of the spouses have a vital role to play. Flexibility of personality leads a couple on to a better, harmonised relationship whereas rigidity is the first step towards the precipice of no-return. Even though such opposing characteristics might seem impossible to merge, yet it is completely possible, and can definitely happen, with a little bit of understanding and patience. Let us look at some of the simple techniques and solutions to bridge the gap across such different personality traits.

Bury the Hatchet Soon

Perception

As a society, we seem to have reached a point in our relationships where words like 'compromise,' 'understanding,' 'trust' etc. are thrown around without any true intent or profound feelings. These words are just that, words, and weigh and convey very little. In real life, a lot of action needs to be taken to truly sustain the value of these words. A lot of work needs to be put in to give relationships a solid foundation. Perceptions between spouses should always continue to be positive even if their individual thoughts or personalities are conflicting. Unless you are aware of both—the strengths and weaknesses of your spouse—which may have genetic, environmental, financial or social origins, you will never be in a position to truly understand your partner. Recognizing these attributes, and realising their effects, can not only alleviate confusions and mollify hurt feelings, but they will also make you more flexible and empathetic. The most obvious outcome of good perception and understanding is better, clearer communication with your partner, and these two, in cohesion, ultimately lead to the Holy Grail of marriage and family: Satisfaction and Happiness.

Communication

Strong, clear and positive interactions and communication between spouses are a necessary counterpart for quality perception. Excellent perception of your spouse's weaknesses and strengths establishes strong bedrock for your relationship. The equally important structure of family values for your child that is built upon this foundation is created mainly by open and honest communication. If husbands and wives mutually respect each other, their communion gets a firm backbone, and becomes a nurturing ground for well-developed children through better communication skills. This is conducive to attaining harmony and peace in relationships.

Negative communication is often characterised by either distorted communication or one-way communication, and is extremely unhealthy. It is a strong indicator of unwillingness and non-co-operation from one or both the spouses.

Distorted communication occurs when spouses regularly bicker and criticize each other, on unfair grounds, and often, on fairly petty matters, and are unwilling to understand or even entertain the other's viewpoints. This turns into a battlefield to prove the might of one's prejudiced and narrow viewpoints over the other's, and only results in destruction and disintegration of the already frayed bonds of the relationship. Since neither spouse is even open to the consideration that the other may have valid arguments, this sort of communication is not only useless, as it fails to transfer any relevant information, it is also harmful because it tends to rubbish and disparage the other's feelings and perspectives.

One-way communication usually involves one spouse, who is constantly argumentative and fault-finding, with the other spouse choosing to keep a firm silence, either due to a sense of intimidation or fear, or due to forced indifference or apathy. This sort of one-sided communication is just as harmful, because there is no mutual exchange of viewpoints, and thus, no room for any kind of constructive arguments or positive reinforcements. Since only one spouse is involved in the conversation, it becomes impossible to find any grounds of reconciliation, with the result that the apathy between the spouses only increases by the day.

Positive communication, on the other hand, is in complete opposition to the wrongs of negative communication. It seeks to establish open, honest relationships through a free exchange of opinions, ideas and even criticisms, between the spouses. It does not mean a complete elimination of arguments or fights; it only seeks to ensure that even arguments can have a positive outcome if you can focus clearly on the reasons and differences, and if both spouses can honestly convey to each other their needs, fears and desires. Positive communication can, of course, only come about when spouses perceive each other's attributes strongly. It seeks to establish a fair and equal exchange of viewpoints, through open channels of communication. This is highly conducive to attaining harmony in relationships and thus becomes one of the essential pre-requisites for the healthy upbringing of children.

A strong relationship can exist only where spouses are free to communicate with each other, without any fear of retribution or ill-will, and they give values to their counterpart's views, ideas and thoughts. Even if they differ at any point, they can easily sort out the disparities and confusions through clear, focused communication. And, once they can clear out their differences and establish mutual respect for each other's perspectives, it is only then that they will be joined in perfect union.

If you perceive and communicate well with your spouse, all the issues which might possibly spark off marital discord can be managed and settled. Put a tick (√) mark against your problem, if you find that it is destroying the quality of your marriage. Realise that these problems are due to inadequate and improper perceptions and communication, enhance your ability of proper perception, and communicate accordingly. Once you learn to do this right, you will be able to put your problems behind you:

- lack of trust;
- lack of transparency;
- communication breakdown;
- disagreement over disciplining your child;
- use of crude or profane language;
- insults made before outsiders or other members of the family;
- disagreements over the nature of expenditure;
- decisions taken singly, without common consensus;
- disagreements over food, clothes etc.;
- forgetfulness over important dates or promises, namely, birthdays, marriage anniversaries, attending parties, movies, or other social events;
- inability to spend time with the family;
- indiscipline: being irregular/late in daily activities;
- inconsideration/indifference to spouse's interests/problems;
- spending too much time with friends and little with family;
- often the worst kind of issue is addiction: drinking, smoking, chewing tobacco, or other sorts of substance abuse.

The above mentioned factors involved lack of trust and openness, improper or no communication, lack of discipline, autocracy, callousness, and different kinds of addictions.

This rift occurs without any proper or significant reason, and spouses begin drifting apart.

When a quarrel takes place between the spouses, a child wants to stop it, but parents shouldn't be judgmental. Some may harbour a false belief that 'my child loves me more than his father/mother'. You may be completely wrong. A child may love even his alcoholic father/mother as much as she loves you. So, to reiterate, parents should not be judgmental on this ground. A child always sees his two progenitors as one—Parents! Your child is not willing to admit faults in any one of the parents, no matter how much you convince your child.

You should take some rational and mutual steps to protect your child from the jolt of marital-discord. Identify the problems first and then start solving them, one by one. There are some real real-life examples of problems which, generally, couples are encountering that make everyone's life miserable.

Take the case of Tanmoy, a twelve-year-old, who kept sobbing and telling me:

'If anybody forces me to go to school, I'll kill myself.' After long persuasion, Tanmoy narrated the reason for his misery: 'I was playing with my friends. All of a sudden I heard my mother screaming for help. I ran towards my house. I found my parents' bedroom was locked. I forced it open. I found my mother against the wall, bleeding and my father hitting her repeatedly. I pushed my father away and he fell on the floor. I took my mother away from him.' After a brief pause he expressed his fear, 'My father will kill her someday. So I have to stay at home and take care of her.'

Tony was underweight and looking very depressed. He was suffering from poor appetite, disturbed sleep and lack of confidence due to the parental discord at home.

When I interacted with his parents, it was quite shocking that they did not have any clue how their problems were affecting their brilliant son and pushing him into a death-wish.

Nikita, Tony's mother, approached me, seeking help on her husband's part.

She narrated her story: "My husband has a tendency to act without any proper cause. His action often comes like a bolt from the blue. I generally lock the door when my husband is in a rage, in order to conceal this unpleasant event from my only son. My husband even hates me to find me keeping myself happy."

Her story was about the difference in their way of living, burdened, as they were, with financial problems. The losses incurred by her husband in business had a deleterious effect on him. He would turn a deaf ear to her pleadings and her opinions. To ensure that this didn't affect her child's growth, she concealed her problems behind a cloak of superficial cheer. This was increasingly becoming her depressive husband's point of objection. And so, the relationship soured.

How she could sort out the whole thing was what she wished to gather from me.

Nikita was playing her part of being a good mother. But could she continue doing so? It was naïve on her part that she hardly knew that her son, Tony, was aware of all the happenings from his childhood and was brooding over them.

Apart from this, Nikita possesses a positive personality and has a pragmatic view of life. Her husband has a negative attitude and an impractical outlook. His mentality stops him being a constructive person. Moreover, Nikita's perception of the problem was strong but she could not convince her husband to appraise the problem in a positive way and work out a solution accordingly; this is simply because on account of her husband's blocked mind with preconceived notions, which prevented him from perceiving and noticing the matters of consequence – essentially concerning him and involving him which call for urgent remedial actions. On the contrary, to exacerbate the situation, he developed jealousy and anger towards her. Here Nikita is like a number of wives with more or less similar case histories.

I would make my own deductions in each case, and try to solve it accordingly. In many cases, the lady of the house is found to handle events and situations by maintaining such a delicate balance as it seems an easy thing to do. The same situation often puts the husband in a corner that makes him aggressive or depressive as a reaction to his inability to solve the riddles of life.

Gradually, as my practice grew, several such cases turned up, speaking volumes about the differences in spouses' dispositions, perceptions and ways of communication.

There are some basic formulae to follow and firm up the marital relationship, so as to leave the bond intact.

The following instance represents the commonest issues between spouses in the modern age:-

Piyush, seventeen years old, was sitting before me. He had run away from his home twice. He was brought to me by his parents. Both the parents were highly educated and held high positions in their respective companies. Piyush had several complaints against his parents. He was facing a psychological trauma due to parental discord since his early childhood. Now he was quite grown up and he wanted to be rid of his parents, and what he uttered in a determined tone was not an unexpected reaction.

Now it's my turn to do what I wish to do! My parents deprived me of the beautiful experiences of childhood. They are the main culprits behind my problems. I will never forgive them. No way! Of course, they did not deprive me of any luxury but their constant arguments ruptured the harmony of the home. Moreover, they have a strange habit that they often stop talking to each other and use me as an intermediary—as if I was a spokesperson who carries messages between them. Isn't it an awful situation for me?'

After listening to his complaints against his parents, I advised him to make a list of his unpleasant experiences from childhood. He prepared a list from when he was eight years old, where after these incidents became a nightmarish experience for him. This list was quite long:-

- The family is often unaware of my father's whereabouts.
- My mother, too, is suspicious about my father.
- My father used to suspect my mother of having an illicit affair.
- My mother took me along to follow my father on his way to his business place.
- My father came to know this and used violence against my mother.

- He ignored her, ill-treated and verbally abused her.

Piyush's parents were shocked to find how their son recalled every incident exactly though he was so much younger then. They admitted their faults but were still repeating the same mistakes. The core finding of this case was that they were inflexible and not coming to terms to accept their frailties (one of the frailties of human nature is laziness), in the interests of each other. Above all, they did not have extramarital affairs but their inability to spend time together gave rise to their mutual suspicions. They were blaming each other and fighting like cats and dogs.

So, parents! Beware! A child, who is a witness to frequent parental discord, will hardly have a normal code of behaviour.

Kids, the real victims

Here was Rohan sitting by his mother across my table with a rare dignity. Intervening in almost each of her remarks, he made due corrections and then passed the questions on to me. This was interesting.

His father, the main culprit in their combined eyes, was an aggressive man. He would often speak vociferously. Though they appeared well looked after, their grievance was that they didn't feel at ease while he was around.

I could make out that Rohan was his natural self while with his mother. He was putting his, or their, point across to me. He was quite uncertain to take any drastic step fearing his father's rejection of the same, and would whine with his mother over petty things as a result. This was a direct outcome of his utter helplessness to put forth his point of view to his father.

Rohan also couldn't contain his anger against his mother, for she would patiently wait for the tide to pass. She found her aggressive husband too tough to handle. Her dependence on him for each one of his odd decisions, felt Rohan, was demeaning.

Parents! Completely independent decisions taken by either of you (generally by the husband, in the Indian set-up) on any matter can become the commonest factor sparking discord. The seriousness of this situation escapes most couples. Rifts in the relationship between the spouses become apparent creating a tense environment in the family where your child is the sole and silent sufferer.

I handled many cases where I found the cause for a male's failure in maintaining a proper relationship was his own set of ideas (again, rigidity). A man often takes it as a birthright to be dominant in his behaviour post-marriage. This attitude grows in him with great pace, as he becomes a parent and the child enters his formative age. This, to an extent, may be helpful as it keeps the child in check and disciplined. However, it is best to tone down the rigidity part and keep it for use in apt situations. There are times when the child needs pure and gentle love of his father and mother. It would be cruel to his upbringing if the child feels afraid to reach up to his aggressive or rigid parent in those times. Parents themselves could be the models to instil and reinforce deviant behaviour, such as aggression, or promote rigidity.

Take a deep breath and ponder over the matter.

Parents! Wake up!

It's hard to know what step your child will take and whether it is going to be detrimental to you and society. How can you afford to see your child on the brink of disaster, e.g., turning into an antisocial element or committing suicide? Aren't you responsible for his antisocial behaviour or his pathetic end?

Parents, if your child is an alcoholic, drug addict or addicted to substance abuse, criminal or gambler, or joins a group which makes him antisocial, your contribution to such behaviour could have been the foremost! It does not matter how innocent you are! It seems harsh but true. Unknowingly, your own problems send a subtle message to your child: 'ESCAPE……,' because he is unable to cope with this unpleasant and non-congenial situation at home. As a result, he is compelled to join the group which gives him solace, albeit in a negative manner. After that, his comeback is almost impossible, or his cruellest step could be to finish himself. If you have been guilty or apathetic, why repent over spilt milk?

Ask yourself:

Why is your child forming a big friends' circle?

Or:

Why is he sitting quietly and having less food and sleep?

A child of the present time is so obsessed with academics that parental discord is something he finds very difficult to tolerate. Your brilliant child cannot go far with this unpleasant emotional load on his back. He will get tired soon. Your own baby plant which you wait for it to blossom will soon wither away. Ultimately, you will have to pay a substantial price for your ignorance and failure. You will never be able to compensate for this setback by any means. Never!

Now, it's time to incorporate some changes in one's interests to meet the demands of the situation. It is imperative to establish strong interpersonal relationships with one's spouse and child.

All one has to do is to recognize one's spouse's interests and make a genuine effort to get involved in them. This flexibility in interests has a good impact on one's own psychological and mental well-being, too.

Tips For The Husband

- Take a break once in a month for your family exclusively.

  It is very important that you realise that your family needs your personal time, which they hate sharing with your friends or others. Do make sure you hand over that much space to them, if only once in a month.
- Waiting for that day is very exciting for your child. They think a great deal about the outing. You will find yourself fulfilled by watching their excitement. Don't deprive your child of this excitement.
- Express your anger when absolutely necessary because you are full of anxiety. But make sure that after some time you explain the reasons for your outburst. Be careful of venting your anger on members of the family because of your failure to solve your official or professional problems.
- Remember: economics is not the only face of the cards you deal in terms of life. Yes, there is importance attached to the money factor, but try cutting it down to a point. Check it—do you tend to dissipate a large amount of energy over small issues?
- Watching TV is a relaxation. But the comfort of being with your spouse and child is even more soothing.
- Finally, just as your quarrels are often in full view of your child, make sure that you do some soft talk as well with your life partner in front of your child.

Many good fathers understand their spouses' interest and accept it, in order to keep the family atmosphere warm and comfortable without making any fuss.

Tips For A Wife

- Keep silent when your husband is verbally aggressive.
- Try not to be the reason for his outbursts. They come due to many external stress-inducing factors (e.g., from the work-place).
- Be cheerful; it may give him the necessary boost to go ahead with life.
- Find a suitable time to talk to your husband.
- Do not nurture the image of your husband as unemotional because males are often more emotional than females. Find out the reasons for his silence. Sometimes he is scared of your reactions. Present your strong and patient side to him so that he feels free to ventilate his feelings, ideas and thoughts. Do not block them. If you have objections, wait for a while and find a suitable time to talk it over. You will see the difference.
- Never form a clique with your children while excluding your husband. This is often a result of the annoyance he may have caused to you.
- Never try to turn your child against his/her father.

For The Spouses

- Make your spouse your best friend, guide and philosopher. Admire him/her. Spend time together at home and outside. It takes time to grow together as friends.
- Always be affectionate with, and fond of, your spouse. Love cannot last without its expression. This is the art of BONDING.
- Remember the important days: birthdays, anniversaries and others. It highlights your caring nature.
- Be transparent with your spouse and talk with him/her always.
- Develop confidence, affection and appreciation for him/her.
- Give him/her a little pleasant surprise quite often. It keeps your love alive and fresh.
- Be sensitive to each other's feelings.

- Recognise and understand your spouse's personality and weaknesses.
- Show genuine interest in your spouse's career and exploits.
- Share any sexual inhibitions that you have with your spouse.
- While dealing with a problem, keep focused on the issue. Address 'what' instead of 'who' is right or wrong.
- Respect each other's privacy.
- Welcome each other's relatives and friends.
- Keep yourself looking good. Attend to personal grooming and maintain the interest of your spouse.
- Be able to assess your mistakes and, where necessary, laugh at yourself sometimes.
- Leave room for the opinions of others.
- Avoid being suspicious, hypersensitive or thin-skinned. Let some comments go by sometimes. Do not respond to everything.
- Avoid feeling insecure when others disagree with you. Allow them to exercise their rights. Try to learn from their disagreements—you might just be surprised to see another solution.
- Make careful considerations and act decisively with preparation for any necessary changes or adjustment.
- Comparing your spouse with others can be detrimental.
- Don't let any other person interfere in your marriage life, except professional advisors/counsellors when needed.
- Avoid using mean, degrading words. Give a careful thought to how you express dissatisfaction or disagreement with her/him.
- Don't be autocratic while making decisions. Believe in mutuality. Respect your spouse's decision.
- Financial planning is crucial. Mutual planning enhances the quality of your family.
- Both of you should be communicative.
- You should solve the problems jointly as much as possible (familial, social, financial, even official).
- Finance, i.e. investments, expenditures etc., should be open to discussion for both of you.
- Make your budget jointly.
- Hiding financial strategy often aggravates the problems.

- You should participate actively and jointly in social activities and follow the rituals.
- If you fight with your spouse in front of the child, make sure to show affection as well; also, convince your child about your spouse's good qualities.
- Never fight in public. It works in the child like slow poison!
- Never use your child as a go-between when both of you stop communicating. It will instill a fear and insecurity in him. As a result, he may start running away from his family in search of emotional compensation.
- Remember! Your quarrels may leave a permanent scar on your child's mind.
- If at first you don't succeed, keep on trying.

It is truly said: "The most important thing a father can do for his children is to love their mother."- Theodre Hesburgh.

In Search of Solace

Sneha was quite upset and wanted some assurance from me so that she could minimize her guilt feelings: "I'm cheating on my husband. I'm involved with a man who gives me a sense of security and satisfies my existence. I'm tired of my husband's verbal attacks. My husband often takes me for granted and behaves with me as if I was devoid of any feelings. Due to my kids and social restrictions I find myself helpless in getting rid of him. I've only one way to satisfy my emotional needs to make male friends outside my marriage. I justify myself for that and find my husband as a culprit..."

Several cases of more or less the same problems and complaints against the spouses are occurring and they accept it without any fear.

In the absence of affection and trust, many spouses are breaking family rules and regulations. Many married people have innumerable complaints against their spouses. This is pathetic! In Indian culture, where divorce is still rare, many remain either in a state of grief or try to find solace outside marriage. Extramarital affairs are on the rise. This is a game of wilful oblivion where a person spends some moments with another and gets a temporary relief by forgetting worries or sharing unhappiness or grievances.

Enquiries with several parents revealed that owing to their high anxiety level they are prone to minimize the dangers of negative mental health by being more of enjoyment- or excitement-seekers. It helps them overlook the state of their own mental health (anxiety, depression, anger etc.): the need for affiliation, attention and fun can largely overcome the impact of negativity in them. The following are general complaints made by the maximum number of wives.

WIFE: 'I'm not getting attention from my husband... He is often busy with his own circle...he behaves with me as if I did not exist....I was a housewife; he hardly bothers about my pocket money. I've to depend on him even for the household expenditure. He provides me a limited amount of money although we don't have financial problems ...He is polite and amiable with his female colleagues...I'm afraid he is having affairs...He comes home late at night...never shows either physical or emotional attachment...I can't take his infidelity any more... he doubts my male colleagues and acquaintances and tortures me...he is very abusive...his drinking habit drives me crazy...either he keeps silent or raises a storm...he never discusses anything with me and does whatever he wants to do...he never shows his bank accounts...I don't get money from him...he seldom goes on any vacations...he has left all responsibilities of our kids solely on me...his work is outside the city and he visits us once in a month for a few days but often spends time with his friends...I'm fed up with his tendency to torment me emotionally ...I want to leave him but due to my child I won't be able to do so.'

HUSBAND: 'My wife is obstinate...I don't trust her...she doesn't take care of me...she is nagging...she lies most of the time...I don't want to stay home...she is demanding...materialistic...does not respect me or attend to my needs...she often argues and is in a mood to quarrel...I find my wife is only concerned with my money and she thinks that I'm spending money on others...She has no trust in me ...she does not respect my parents, siblings, friends, colleagues or staff. She insults me before them intentionally...her shopping mania causes irritation ...she gives more importance to her kitty parties and friends than her family...she does not value time... makes endless phone calls...talks to her friends... treating me as a worthless creature...she lacks emotions and a caring attitude...she often finds faults with me...... .'

Some of the wives revealed their feeling of insecurity and inadequacy. They added: 'I then try to find solace in others' company.'

The mother's depression and the child's behavioural disorders characterise those families where the mother has been abused by her spouse and has the tendency to keep her feelings to herself or seek the company of others where she feels secured.

Thus a shift of emotional fulfilment from the spouse to another person is common in both the spouses. If a spouse fails to cater to the emotional longing of their counterpart it may adversely affect the stability of the family, because the need for attention is as important as other needs, e.g., food, water, sex, etc. People with anxiety and depression may seek enjoyment to maintain their state of well-being by getting attention outside marriage. This trait opens up avenues for feeling excitement, thrill and the need for one's own pleasure through emotional interactions which may threaten the congenial home atmosphere. This enjoyment may include a cocktail party, intimate relationship with the opposite sex, shopping mania, kitty party, and so on.

In a number of cases, it is observed that some spouses (especially males) who are anxious due to financial constraints, insecurity, lack of family cooperation, debts etc., try to maintain their ego and status and are found to avoid or escape from real-life situations by being more fun-loving outside the home and indulging in behaviour involving thrill and risk such as gambling, betting, drinking, smoking, and quick means of making money. Perhaps this gives them a transient pleasure and relief from the day-to-day demands of life which leave them anxious and depressed.

In fact, all the aforesaid forms of behaviour are a reflection of one's own anxiety, insecurity, inferiority complex and fear of failure which may induce a higher degree of insecurity in their children.

The negative and conflicting personality patterns of parents affect the child's perception of the parents and contribute to their behavioural problems, as I observed during my interview sessions with the parents.

The child seems to feel an emotional distance from both the parents which leaves him hungry for attachment and love.

Your child interprets every movement of yours in his/her own way. So, parents, be careful about your child's perception of you as a parent and as an individual, too!

DIVORCE

Thirteen-year-old Aman broke down and divulged in a distressed voice, "My parents are very selfish…they think only about their own happiness…they never ask what I want….they may start living separately very soon….I can't leave any one of them. They often quarrel regarding my possession but they don't know what's going on in my mind. But I'm sure I need both of them."

His piercing eyes had an expression as if I would do some miracle for him. There are lots of Amans who are going through a severe psychological trauma due to parental severance. No kid likes this indivisible human shelter on the earth. It is a fact!

Many kids viewed, "Divorce is a selfish decision taken by the parents only for their own convenience. They lack compassion for their children."

This is the rebellious attitude of children who are going through the trauma of their parents' divorce.

Parents!

Divorce is an extremely sensitive issue. You definitely cut a sorry figure for your children if you do so. To do justice with this special relationship you have to exert your maximum effort to keep this valuable relationship alive.

"Curriculum problems can be solved by hard work. Can you solve my family problems…especially my parents' dispute??"—fourteen-year-old Jishu's ambivalent feelings (love-hate) towards his parents were quite evident on his face. But he soon changed and surrendered himself and told me, "Let them fight but tell them not to get separated. I need both of them." Jishu was looking at me with a great hope. He again reminded me of sweet Kaka. From Kaka's time till today: the percentage of literacy is on the rise, and simultaneously there is the rise in the percentage of incompetent parenting and parents' own selfish attitude. However, Jishu represents thousands of children who never want to see their creator in two pieces.

After interviewing a number of couples, who were blaming each other, without a real or valid ground, through and through, I find that their discord covers:

- lack of transparency;
- communication disturbances;
- personality differences;
- incompatibility;
- dishonesty with finances;
- lack of respect; and
- burden of joint family.

All the above mentioned grounds are very much repairable if you tackle them carefully.

A renowned person, Mr X came to me to reveal his inferiority complex due to his wife's rural upbringing and culture, which was obviously in contrast with his own. It was shocking that he did not want to accompany her to any party or even in public places due to her lack of glamour, attraction and charm. As a result, he was seeking divorce.

Another renowned person, Mr Y, came to me to reveal his difficulties in getting along with his wife due to his wife's urban culture, even when he himself had a popular existence. Still he felt insecure and often stayed in a state of despondency and avoided parties and public places due to his wife's glamour, attraction and charm. It was also moving towards divorce.

The agonies of both the couples are the same but in contrasting ways.

In both the cases the couples are insecure, sad and lack insight. Both the couples are not happy and thinking on the lines of divorce.

Divorce on this ground shows immaturity and shallowness of the knowledge of family and social union. First of all, this diversity in personality is not a problem. It shows your own complexes and avoidance to meet the family commitments.

If you are committed to the family responsibilities affably, these problems may vanish soon.

In order to cultivate the interests/hobbies which your spouse is having, it does not matter whether it is related to rural or urban culture because a "family" itself is a respected place and you will get lots of respect and honour if you have a beautiful family bonding. You will soon find how your spouse comes forward and willingly accepts your hobbies, too, if you cooperate with him/her. Do not escape. Bind a beautiful union between the the two of you: it hardly matters whether your spouse is outspoken, glamorous or rustic and lacks a refined etiquette and manner. Your support, love and cooperation are enough to bind him/her with you.

Although divorce is the outcome of a mutual agreement between the spouses, its impact on their kids cannot be overlooked.

Does your spouse abuse/cheat, and have you lost trust?

Do you think financial secrecy is the crux of your problem?

Talk quietly. Be a forgiving person.

Trust sometimes breaks so divorce may not be the only answer. There is surely something missing in your conjugal life. Find out what it is. Bring it back. After all, we are human beings, we make mistakes. Be a great person by being forgiving and forgetting. Do not be a mean person by brooding over the problem. It will ruin any relationship.

There are some suggestions for the spouses (with kids) which may be beneficial prior to the happening of divorce:

Make sure: Will you get rid of your problems by getting rid of your spouse?

Because, many a time, a person is trapped in the illusion that if he/she gets rid of the spouse they will get rid of their problems, too. You have to be honest enough while you are assessing your life 'with the spouse' or 'without the spouse' by taking into account your kid(s), too. Do not allow your ego to interfere with this sensitive issue. It is seen that in most of the cases one's ego is the main culprit behind this devastating break in relationship.

Do the following work:

Make a list of pleasant and unpleasant happenings of your life before saying goodbye to your spouse. Weigh logically and then decide.

Will the post-divorce status render you a set of new personality traits?

Will you change yourself by getting rid of your spouse? Ask yourself silently. You may get your answers.

If the relationship is unbearable, talk logically and convincingly to your child without making much fuss.

If you talk against your spouse with your child, certainly you are breaking your child's heart. You may have feeling of satisfaction or you feel that you are saving your side by being not a culprit and you want to prove yourself 'not guilty' in the eyes of your child but you are hurting your child at the other end with your self-deceptive attitude and erroneous course of action. They are vulnerable to stress and may try to find solace in drugs, alcohol or any other forbidden or thrilling thing or drastic step to make up the setback. It is better to counsel your child personally than taking anyone else's help, like a family member or friend.

If the divorce is inevitable, part gracefully.

Divorce is advisable under life-threatening situations. In case of parents with alcohol addiction, drug addiction and severe personality disorder where one's life is really in danger, it is advisable to take divorce.

Shikha, a fourteen-years-old girl, was trembling with shock and fear while she was narrating her parents' violence due to her father's alcoholism and she wanted to get rid of them. She was also worried about the security of her parents. She was wishing for her parents to start living separately as soon as possible.

I was dealing with the problems of wives in a group session. The topic was: Mechanism of Behaviour. Some wives were sad, depressed and confused, while others were angry and hostile due to their husbands' adamant attitudes, carelessness, self-centredness, negligence, indifference and even drinking problems and pathetic dependence on substance abuse.

Renuka was worried about her husband's demanding nature. She confided in me (in her own version) as follows:

'My husband is not at all considerate when family issues come up, he never compromises even on food and clothes; he wants the child and me to obey him at once, any delay means a big row. So we obey him quietly. His decision is final and irrevocable. Above all, his drinking problem is making the situation worse. He does what he likes. He hardly gives us money and we always suffer from financial insecurity. How long can this go on?'

After listening to her, Ankur, Renuka's husband, who was looking pale and older than his years, was ready to cooperate with me because he really needed to solve his overbearing problems. He said:

'I find myself helpless. I want to work hard but I can't stay away from alcohol. I know my weakness but I can't overcome it. I am trying hard to leave this habit but in vain. I'm desperate now.'

After reviewing the situation, I decided to give some theoretical information to Ankur. I decided that any sort of preaching was not going to work with this helpless creature. I started my talk:

'Look! You should know about your inner mechanisms first. It may provide you some vital insights into your desires and needs. It may help you understand why a human being is helpless before his lust and desires, in spite of being so powerful. Only human beings can control many aspects compared to other creatures. If you understand the inner mechanisms and apply them logically in your life, you can be a winner.'

Ankur is representative of a community which is helpless in correcting their unethical and undesirable needs, like alcohol, drugs, betting, gambling and other activities (including perhaps sexual harassment/molestation or even rape).

I tried to explain it to Ankur through the theory of Freud, one of the giants in the field of psychology. Psychological surgery or surgery of the mind sometimes does wonders.

A person, who wants to gratify his own desires immediately, irrespective of moral values and norms, is usually motivated by the instinct which is known as 'Id'; if it is prominent in him he hardly cares for others' sensitivity and even unaware of the drastic consequences of his actions. He wants to fulfil it by hook or by crook. Many criminals, gamblers, alcoholics, substance abusers, killers, rapists and those who create terror constantly are guided by their id instinct only.

Ankur was looking puzzled but seeking some solutions when he asked,

'How can I get rid of my drinking problem?'

I tried to encourage him,

'Well! This is tough but not impossible. In many cases, it was found that if a person accepts and understands the facts, he tries to change himself. But the problem with such a person is that he avoids or gets irritated by others' advice due to his utter rigidity or you may say, strongly governed by his Id mechanism. Because a person who is driven by the Id instinct only finds himself helpless to reform; hence, many addicts and criminals lack the insight of correcting themselves. However, there are many examples of people who corrected themselves by developing the correct insight.'

Ankur looked quite enthusiastic in knowing the psychological mechanisms of human beings and saw a ray of hope. I continued my talk on the mechanisms described by the Freud,

'Look! An important part of the mind in a human being is the Ego. This is related to Reality theory. The function of the Ego is to control the demands and desires of a person aroused by the Id. As the Ego has the practical link with the external world so it works as a mediator between the desires of the Id and the realities of the world. It gives an insight into how being impulsive or selfish can hurt one's feelings and affect one's family in the long run. Once this insight develops in you, you may react like, "Oh! It's the Ego's job to meet the needs of the Id…let me take the help of this mechanism. Is this the Id who is misguiding me? Is it overpowering me? No, no! I can't be the slave of the Id." It may take time but after realization one may start working on that line. This is called, self-assurance. By assuring yourself you can develop a positive will-power which is the only tool on the globe through which you can follow the right path. '

Priyanka, a 35-year-old lady, who also joined the group session, looked sad and reacted differently, but fearlessly spoke of her problem:

"My husband, Subodh, had been drinking for many years. He used to be very adamant and self-centred and his tantrum often vitiated the environment of our family. Good food was the main pleasure of his life.

He never compromised on his eating and drinking habits. He had no consideration for his family. But all of a sudden he stopped drinking and started taking simple food. It was not a withdrawal symptom. I now observe that he often talks about idealism and super power. He has lost interest in many things. He wants to be a 'sanyasi'. He often keeps silence, although he looks perfectly normal; no sign of madness is visible because his routine is not affected at all and he also works as usual. His behaviour is making my children and I feel very insecure. I find myself alone while dealing with the family complexes. It has a bad effect on my kids. They are always scared of their father's changed mood. Why does he behave so?"

I wanted to relate the third sub-system, the Super Ego, of Freud:

'See! Priyanka, There is another part of the mind which operates through a person's behaviour. And this is the "Super ego" which is based on morals, values and ideals. It warns a person about what is right and wrong. It conveys the message to the Ego about what is immoral and unethical. But when it operates singly, without the Id and the Ego, it sometimes leads a person towards a high idealism which is still detrimental to a pleasant family life. Valmiki of ancient time is one of the examples; initially, he was solely motivated by his Id drive and used to loot and rob the people but when he detached himself from that drive he came under the influence of the Super ego which turned him into a Maharshi (Yogi) and he became a legendary author by writing the epic *Ramayan*. If a *Grihastha* (family man) comes under the influence of this super ego, it sometimes may be taken as an indicator of escape from the responsibilities of family life. Because the family man is committed to fulfilling the needs and desires of the family, the impact of the super ego may be inimical to a congenial home environment. Thus a person who is guided by only the Id or the Super-ego may have a tendency to escape from the realities. Making him aware of this fact may turn him into a responsible person.'

Thus, these three intra-psychic subsystems, viz. Id, Ego and Super-ego are of crucial importance in determining one's behaviour. Frustrations, anxiety, depression and anger often set in when a person is unable to resolve conflicts among the Id, Ego and the Super-ego. When you have provided a fine tuning to each and every part of your inner sub-systems, you will explore yourself much more convincingly. You can exercise your self-control comfortably and discover your limitations, too.

After a few months, Ankur contacted me with a fresh smile. He was looking quite confident and lively. He was thankful to me but my vision got a new dimension and I thought that he had been able to grasp the theory practically. Although he did not leave the alcohol completely, yet he started taking it very occasionally. He discovered a new world after getting rid of his addiction.

Priyanka convinced her husband to join the counselling sessions. Subodh has now started actively participating in social activities and the household chores.

Frustration is an outcome of poor problem-solving skill in spouses. Most spouses are the victims of adjustment disorder due to their poor coping-style and problem-solving traits. If they start exploring the reasons behind their addictions, indulgence, strife, discords and adjustment-disorder, logically they will surely find a way of dealing with the problems rationally without rupturing the harmony of the family. If they fail to do so the problems will aggravate and may take an ugly form which you have never imagined. Watch the circumstances meticulously.

❑❑❑

PART-III

The Child : A Silent Perceiver

- *Parenting Styles: Working Mother to a Single Parent*
- *Solution & Tips*

Come Back to the Child's Perception

Sometimes, parents are unaware of the harm they may do to themselves, as well as to their child, with their words and actions. Their child may not be a brilliant performer at school, but the parents seem to be mired in a false sense of pride. They brag about their child's performance in their circle even when they may have failed in a number of subjects.

In lots of social gatherings, it is pathetic to hear the conversations and discussions of parents who hold a high place in society. The child's performance becomes a prestige issue for them. They find the child's failure to be a sort of social stigma. I observed that these kinds of parents are more worried about their own prestige and less concerned about their child's career.

'My parents have such high expectations from me that it scares me— what if I fail to live up to them? It seems that I have to study not for myself, but for my parents and relatives'—the view of an eleven-year-old girl Lisa who had attempted suicide.

Shubham, a thirteen-year-old boy, who represents numerous children's dilemma, was telling me about his parents' expectations: 'I'm really confused between my career and my parents' expectations.'

Sometimes, parents lie without considering its impact on their child's mind. Parents usually do not realise that when they brag about their child, their innocent child silently watches how they lie about them. Children fail to identify themselves with the parents and they think it is their duty to secure good marks—by hook or by crook. As a result, they adopt various kinds of unfair means during examinations; if they fail in a subject they sign the report card by counterfeiting their parents' signature(s) , they run away from home, or, in some high-stress cases, they even attempt or commit suicide.

Minu, an eight-year-old girl, was trembling with fear because she had been caught red-handed while cheating in her final examinations: 'My parents will beat me if I fail...my cousins often get good marks...' She was muttering in distress.

Her anxious face revealed how much stress and pressure she was carrying on her shoulders due to her parental expectations and demands.

Let's have a quick glance at the complaints of children against their parents:

— High and unrealistic expectations.

— They chat about our performances and achievements with their relatives and friends.

— They quarrel among themselves related to our issues, and, ultimately, they end up involving us.

— They are too busy to be able to spend much time with us.

— Many of my parents' friends are drinkers and smokers.

— They get angry on seeing my report card even though they never check on me or my school work.

— They are seldom present at my school functions.

Often, children have a lot to complain about their mother:

— My mother is busy with her friends, in kitty parties or shopping.

— She is a working mother but when she's at home, she shouts at me most of the time.

— She always leaves me in with carers , and doesn't have enough time for me.

— My mother often insults me before my friends.

— Whenever I needed her help I found her sleeping. Sometimes I become very depressed to see my mum asleep after taking sleeping pills.

— I become desperate when my mum takes alcohol and starts ranting; and sometimes I have to calm her down.

— Her eyes are always glued to the computer. Her favourite pastime is to chat on Facebook. When I want to do the same she raises a storm.

A large section of children, especially in the age group of seven to eighteen years, have such common complaints about their parents. This is the time when a child really needs emotional, psychological and physical protection, support and security.

A brief list of child's bitter perceptions about their parents:

— Parents' expectations and their habit of boasting;

— Parents at loggerheads;

— Disapproval of the peer groups of parents cause: alcohol, tobacco, profane language, late night party etc.;
— Making unrealistic demands, insulting, beating, scolding and/or discouraging their behaviour;
— Indifferent and cold towards them the children generally perceive that parents neglect and/or reject them;
— Parents' self-centredness (leading to depression) and their own enjoyment (excitement-seeking behaviour).

The role of the both parents is more or less similar. However, there are some needs of a child which can be catered for by each parent exclusively . In general, a mother provides internal requirements whereas a father introduces the external world.

Caring Mother

The mother's caring nature and gentle attitude helps the child interact comfortably with her without the apprehension of being reprimanded, and the child feels free to interact with her. In such an open environment, even if the child commits a mistake, they always look for mom's guidance. Being cared for, emotionally, psychologically and physically, is the basic need of a child from birth.

The maternal characteristics of emotional warmth and parenting strategies such as loving, caring and good communication play a crucial role in the development of the child's cognition.

The child often needs comfort through the positive parenting of the parents, particularly mothers, so that they can convey their innermost feelings to her, e.g., the parents allow the child to give their suggestions on issues related to family matters or concerning themselves (parents), take care of the child's feelings and desires, and accept the constructive criticism made by the child and guide the child on his wrongful assertions requiring corrective actions. This freedom and liberty provided by the parents to their child fosters self-confidence in their child, as a result, the latter finds themselves more secure and satisfied.

Spending maximum time with a child makes the child feel protected and motivated.

Sharing feelings and experiences with a child fills the child with feelings of being needed and wanted.

The child's perception of their mother as protecting, loving and caring for implies that the positive personality characteristics in the mother make the child feel protected, and cared for. A mother may have positive personality traits, which include, inter alia, the following:-

Her ability to organise, her sense of duty, and preparedness to deal with the problems of life often set a standard for a good quality of parenting to her child, and, as a sequel to all this, the child perceives stability and dependability in their mother, and this instils a feeling of security because of the predictability of her behaviour. This gives rise to a strong and healthy relationship between the mother and child.

Discipline and a sense of duty are the parameters of the stable personality of a mother. They enable the child to perceive their mother positively. Accordingly, this stability of the mother induces in the child the habit to reciprocate positive emotional feedback to their mother.

When a child finds their mother as non-demanding and non-rejecting, this is supposed to be an index of the acceptance of the child by the mother. This positive notion of the child makes the child proud to identify himself with his mother and to feel motivated to internalize the given social values and norms.

Father: As a Knowledge Provider

The father is often the primary figure who helps his child by introducing them to the outer world and forming a real picture of the world outside, which enables a child to develop an independent personality and take rational decisions which will stand them in good stead in the long run. A father in the Indian set-up is generally considered to be more knowledgeable in respect of money matters, banking, and finance as well as human nature. It is observed in a number of cases that fathers treat their offspring as little children even when they grow up. As a result, the child becomes demanding and if their demand remains unfulfilled they show frustration in a number of negative ways. Most importantly, when a child grows up, they initially face a lot of problems in settling down even at their workplace. This may persist in the long run as well. It is found that fathers are often secretive about money matters and they have a wrong notion that discussing financial issues with their child may lead them to be more demanding or it may lead them astray. What I have observed in a number of cases, especially where the fathers are rich, is that they are reluctant to share the state of their finances and accounts even with their grown-up sons. This is very surprising. In such cases, a child has no clue about the financial status of the father and the child spend money recklessly. But even rich fathers may have their burdens, liabilities, and debts, and there may be limitations in declaring the source of the money as well. A child without the requisite financial knowledge may be more prone to being extravagant. A child should learn the management of finance from early childhood. It helps them in the long run, yet many fathers remain totally unaware of this fact.

The mother stands as an emotional guard and the father as a practical guide. It is important for both these figures to realise that academic pressure often does more harm than good, and ends up creating negative perceptions in the child. A person with a well-rounded personality can always end up becoming successful in any field.

Be careful! Your one-time punishment may overshadow your good parenting style.

- A negative parenting style is an inadvertent expression of the mother or father who is worried and fearful regarding the future of her/his child (Overprotection).
- Parents' greater negative parenting, despite being moderated by the positive side, adversely exerts influence over the child's perception of parents (Neglect and Rejection).
- Parenting skill is the most salient ingredient of an effective parenting programme. It is essential for parents to give importance to the art of communication and parenting skills which automatically get reflected in their behaviour and are conveyed to the child pleasantly, positively and in a consistent way.
- **Let us analyse why your 'positive' parenting style leaves no positive impact on your child.**

1. You are showering love and affection on your children.
2. You consider yourself a good parent by being progressive and liberal.
3. You give them good suggestions all the time.
4. You escort them protectively whenever they go out.
5. You think giving your children freedom and space is good for them.

6. You scold or give verbal or corporal punishment to your child, because you think that it is the best way of handling a child.
7. You love your child so much as it is impossible for you to say no when they ask for something.
8. You want to make your child a disciplined civilian by forcing them to do whatever you say.
9. You think that a child will himself/herself learn some day so you do not need to correct them.
10. You are submissive and permissive; so it is hard for you to stop your child when they behave in an undesirable way. In fact, parents of these days are so confused and at a loss in selecting the right method of parenting that they start to apply the methods which are convenient for them or based on their own reasoning. A mother may love and take care of her child properly but her one-time punishment – maybe in the form of slapping, hitting, beating – induces stress and fear in her child, as several researchers concluded (Webster-Stratton).

This negative perception, in turn, generates and reinforces in the child a negative behavioural pattern for the parents. This is why the parental characteristics of emotional warmth and the mutual expressions of loving, caring and satisfying communication have been shown to play a crucial role in the development of a child's cognition. Internalization of parental values helps decrease deviance in children and fills their requirement to derive a stable behavioural pattern from the parents to feel safe and secure.

Unfortunately, the parents' positive behaviour is often contaminated with their negative behaviour. For example, you might show your love to your child several times a day by praising and encouraging them but your one-time punishment, out of your own frustration and discomfiture, may overshadow all the preceding praises showered by you. This is what is called inconsistent parenting.

However, the parents want to rear their child in a positive direction but their shallow knowledge of parenting puts them in a disadvantage and they follow some self-made theory blindly without considering the impact of it on their own child. A child who is watching silently and helplessly the actions, reactions and behavioural pattern of their parents, with lack of indepth knowledge of parental care, has nothing to say. As a result, frustration and aggression start piling up. When the cumulative frustrations cross the threshold, the child becomes restless and looks for a suitable time to release his pent-up feelings. Now on the question arises: where will the child release his accumulated frustrations? The answer is: Mothers should guide the child to engage in useful and constructive activities, and channelize the energy gainfully—instead of resorting to destructive acts.

That is why it is said: A mother is the World!

How to deal with a child having a difficult temperament?

The upbringing of a child becomes tougher when their temperament is negative (rigid, disobedient, throwing tantrums, latent aggression, and withdrawal). There are many young children who can be difficult at times, and whom even good parents can fail to tackle well. During my interview sessions, I came across a lot of parents who said that they spent a considerable amount of time with their children and paid full attention to them, but they were still finding themselves incapable of managing them.

In fact, a child with a negative temperament does not need much attention or extra care; their wish is to perceive a peaceful ambience. On many occasions, it is found that a child, who is, by temperament, rigid and disobedient thinks a lot, makes his own judgments and revolts if somebody interferes with his thought process. A child with this temperament usually needs support, not interference. In such a case, parents should be cautious while applying their parenting style. Their frequent attempts at reforming the habits of their child go in vain—as reported by several mothers. Here, parents' own negative characteristics multiply the problems of their child. Analogous to the situation where person wearing a black glass sees everything in black colour, viewed through the negative characteristics of the child's parents—who are in constant conflicts inter se—the affected child sees only a gloomy picture everywhere.

The following examples show ***how different mothers react differently in the same situation*** after a quarrel between the parents and their child:

Mother-1 to her child: Look! You saw how your dad behaved with me? He has no time even for you! That's why I dislike him' (denigrates it).

Mother-2 to her child: Don't worry! It's a way of life. We can't stay without quarrelling (laughs it away).

There is a big difference in the analysis of the fathers' behaviour done by the mothers. Mother-1 showed her lower tolerance whereas Mother-2 took it easily and comfortably.

Why so?

Mother-2 had a clear perception about her spouse. She knew that his temper/tantrum is the result of his feeling of insecurity and his own shortcomings. Moreover, she had clarity of thought that their momentary outburst may have a disastrous effect on their child if she had shown counter aggression. So she behaved cleverly. Her perception about the child's temperament shows how skilfully she acted while his father lost his temper/threw tantrums.

The need for attachment is not restricted to an early age only, for it continues in adulthood also.

Parenting: A long journey

Depression, anxiety, excitement-seeking behaviour, and maladjustment of parents create a model for the child to observe and learn socially inappropriate behaviour and assimilate it with their own. This learnt and acquired behaviour of a child gradually becomes a part of their personality. Thus perhaps it is not only parental characteristics but the child's disposition which could also be an important determinant to evaluate interpersonal relationships in adulthood. The need for attachment is not restricted to early age only, but it continues in adulthood, too. So a child needs love and affection, off and on, even as a grown-up.

A large number of parents reported about their son (or daughter, as the case may be):'Now he is in the higher classes. He has achieved his career aim. He is satisfied. I don't have any problems. I'm free from my responsibilities. He does not need my guidance at all.'

On the other side of the spectrum, there are many cases of suicide reported from renowned technological institutes. Drug-addiction, alcoholism and other criminal activities are common practice with students studying even in prestigious institutions. Blaming only academic pressure will not reverse this unhappy trend. A few years back, in a reputed engineering college divorced parents were quarrelling over the dead body of their son (who had committed suicide in the hostel): the issue was, who would get possession of their son's dead body? How can we label it as academic stress?

I found the following complaints from hostel children:

- "I don't want to go back home even in the vacations. I can't take the attitude of my parents who often talk to me against each other."
- "Whenever I go back home, I feel like there is no one to understand me. Both my parents are busy and they hardly have time for me."
- "I don't want to watch the suffering of my mom whom my father often abuses. I feel inclined to do something for my mom but my anxiety is so high that I hardly concentrate on my studies. I doubt whether I'll pass."
- "My father has no time for me. I tried to seek suggestions from him but he seems indifferent and busy either with his friends or business. Whenever he is at home, he is only speaking on his phone."
- "My parents are very much self-centred and they think they have done their duty by getting me admitted to a technological institute. They are often busy with cocktail parties and talking highly about me, which I consider a shame. Because they have no time to listen to me, I personally don't approach them. Though I want to confide in them how I'm going through a bad time in the institute. How I'm trapped in a group of alcoholics..."

❑❑❑

Golden Rules

How to be A Competent Parent

Sandhya was confident about her parenting style when she said, "I don't think I neglect my son. But his eating habit makes me crazy sometimes. He wastes a lot of time while eating. A considerable part of my time is directed to persuade him to take the same cooked food that is made for the other members of the family. He is very fastidious regarding his food. If I don't serve food according to his choice he won't be ready to eat. I have to cook for him separately else he prefers to have junk food."

All of a sudden, Piyush jumped up angrily from his chair and grabbing his mother's hand, told me excitedly, 'You know! My mom always insists upon me to eat whatever she cooks, and she cooks whatever she likes. She is forcing me to eat most of the time. Sometimes, to the pitch of disgust (ad nauseam). I feel like vomiting but she will compel me to eat.'

Sandhyaa started shouting, 'Leave my hand! Behave yourself!' Piyush's grip got tighter.

She gave him a slap across his cheek and pushed him aside with force.

She screamed at the top of her voice, 'Can't you admit that you waste your time and my time as well when you eat?'

I was quietly watching the scene and wondering how a mother treats a small issue in such a destructive way. Sandhya's ' action reminded me of Kaka's episode.

Finally, I talked to her as if I was talking to Kaka's mother. 'Sandhya! The sad part is that parents are not aware of how their own behaviour exerts influence upon their child's behaviour. The child's personality is the outcome of the discipline, education or participation with his parents in every aspect of growing-up. How you deal with him becomes an accepted way of dealing for the innocent child. A child picks up the behaviour quickly and incorporates it in his personality as if it was a desirable way to behave. Remember, he has to carry these learnt traits for a lifetime. Your child may end up with adjustment disorder when he reaches adulthood.'

Sandhya: 'Well! I'm doing all these things from the point of view of his health. If I leave him half-fed he may fall sick. It becomes very difficult especially during school time. He has to get ready early and catch his school bus. He always throws a tantrum over his food.'

I told her, 'There are many ways to handle these petty problems. You can convince him to do the things in a fixed time. Never fight over the eating habit. Your duty is to provide the food of his choice, —of course, provided it is healthy. If he refuses, let him go hungry. Do not provide any junk food before school. You may convince him that if he finishes his food you will give him any fast food he likes as a reward. If he again refuses, stop nagging. You practise it for one week and you will certainly get the desired result.'

When I talked to Sandhya I found her stubborn on her own points and it took lots of effort to convince her. She was tired of her son's obstinacy and tantrums, but hesitated to scrutinize her own issues.

Sandhya was looking different when she came after a few sessions,

'A miracle! My son is doing well. At least, his making a fuss over food has stopped. He eats healthy food with a hope to get a reward. I was positively adamant on this issue. I used to coax him saying how much I love him. I do not want to see him sick. Moreover, I conveyed to him that it is better to starve than to have bad food all the time. I explained the difference between starvation and staying on the unhealthy food. It took some days. I used to watch him starving for long hours. Ultimately, he could understand why his mom is so cruel. Now I tell him how much I love him, that's why I was so strict. It is the sign of love not cruelty.'

When I talk to the mother of an eight-year-old child, Rumy, I face plenty of problems in convincing her, like, 'Make a separate bed for your daughter!' They are flabbergasted.

They challenge me, "How will the girl get emotional bonding then?

I suggest again, 'If you have a spare bedroom, even go for that.'

'Emotional bonding' does not happen through sheer sharing of the same bed. It is a warm feeling of affection. You are right about this, but you perceive it in your conservative way. Many parents do not know that sleeping in the same bed makes their child less confident, fearful and even pathetically dependent. Moreover, there are many other ways to establish emotional bonding between the two of you.'

Nidhi, a young mother, who was also participating in the interaction session, jumps up, 'Hurray! I do it. I always had a guilty feeling, whether I'm doing injustice to my daughter.'

'Do you sleep with her for some time? Do you sing her a lullaby? Do you kiss her? Do you wait for her till she sleeps?' I enquired.

'I do. Sometimes she talks a lot and she doesn't let me go. It takes long hours …'

' Nidhi! Avoid talking to your baby while she is about to fall asleep. Lullaby is the best option at that time. Talk and stories are heard by them seriously. It increases their curiosity. They want it more and more. Lullaby is music which doesn't need much attention. Go ahead with it.'

'My child is mostly interested in stories. What will I do?' Nidhi looks dissatisfied.

'Well! You keep some other time for telling stories. What about during meals? That time let them eat by themselves and you start telling them some kind of story. Mealtime is the toughest time for the children. You parents make it out as if a big war was going on between the two of you. Isn't it? So a story may help in reducing the tension. You can use your skill at that time to make your story somewhat realistic or funny as well. It depends on the age of your child. Right education starts from the dinner table, Nidhi! Be a mother who does right things.'

She was looking very happy and she uttered, 'How small things make our child so mischievous—now I can guess!'

"Nidhi! Parents often forget that a child has to carry his early traits for a lifetime, resulting in adjustment disorder in later years. So we parents are very much responsible in sowing the toxic seeds in their immature minds. Then what will be the use of crying over spilt milk?"

Identify the causes of your child's negative behaviour as early as possible, and try to take corrective actions promptly. Let us observe a child's undesirable behavioural problem.

A teenaged child's problem

1. What is the root cause of his/her behavioural problem?
2. What is your reaction?
3. How do you show your displeasure?

4. What is the counter-reaction?
5. Does it turn into a big argument?

You, usually, have arguments over your child's demands for or inclination towards use of a mobile phone, Internet surfing, television addiction, going out, having a large peer group, friendship with the opposite sex, rash driving, late-night partying, bingeing on food, drinking, smoking, and experiencing sex.

There is a simple method to solve all of this: BE YOUR CHILD'S BEST FRIEND, GUIDE AND PHILOSOPHER!

There are, of course, certain methods you have to adopt in trying to form a trusting and transparent relationship with your child.

Be friendly with your child's friends. Encourage your son/daughter to invite them to your place and even arrange parties for your child, if he/she so desires. Be friendly with their parents as well and ensure that you have their phone numbers and addresses and are on good terms with them.

A child finds his own vocation when given a chance to intermix with his age group. So it is always advisable to leave them in company, even to find a companion for the child if he feels too shy to socialize. Your child's shortcomings will be more visible in the presence of others just as lightning flashes clearly against the backdrop of a black sky. These will add vital brownie points to your CV.

Now, if you find that your child's friends are proving to be detrimental to his healthy psychological growth, discuss it with your child. But it is imperative to make sure that you are not judgmental or overtly disapproving of his choice of friends. Give space to your child to realize this fact himself/herself. If you start nagging him/her, it will only end up enhancing your child's desire to maintain that friendship.

Allow your child to spend time on the mobile or for Internet surfing. However, talk to him/her sensibly. If you are aware of your child's friends, you do not need to worry as much. Your pleasant and supportive relation compels him/her to reveal their thoughts and feelings and ensures a healthy and trusting relationship.

Checking the mobile use and emails of your child only leads to spoiling your child's trust in you. Be careful!

This will also help you have excellent and clear discussions with your child regarding unsafe practices such as smoking, drinking, drugs etc.

Your emotional involvement with your child will play a significant role in preventing him/her from becoming the victim of addictions.

Curiosity about sex is normal and, moreover, it is a biological need. It has always been a big issue for parents regarding their children. But be wary: being too suspicious may only end up further pushing them in this direction. If he satisfies his curiosity by surfing the Internet or watching television, you should consider this outlet as normal. If he falls in love with someone, do not consider it as a crime. Nevertheless it is against good principles of morality and incongruous for a student of fall in love. Understand him and his feelings. Stand by their side so that they can discuss this delicate issue with YOU…their best friend, philosopher and guide! So be receptive! Listen!

Parents! Do you know the cause of your child's rash driving? It is a manifestation of your child's frustrations. Frustration in the child today may be over many things considered nonsensical from the parental point of view but they may be crucial from your child's assessment. You have to work it out very sensibly. Do not double his aggression. Be a good listener!

Do not react to his tantrums. Counter-aggression only aggravates his aggression. Give him some space to realize the situation. He will come to you on his own. Wait a little longer!

Identify/modify your communication/miscommunication with your child:

Mother: "Hey! It's 7 o'clock, when will you start your studies?" Child: "But I'm feeling sleepy."

Mother: (loudly) "Get up! Don't forget it's your study time, after that you've to leave for your school."

Child (shouts at the top of her voice): "Go away! …"

This scene shows that a child's morning starts with an unwelcome task, i.e., STUDY.

Parents! Why don't you adopt some pleasant method to wake your child up? How about this: "Darling! We're back from our morning walk.

Come on! Let's have a cup of tea/milk together."

You may get this type of response:

"I've already woke up mom! Waiting for you to come back."—Sounds cheerful.

Parents! Your gentle (but firm and positive) behaviour and moderation make your child more disciplined.

Scene at lunch/dinner time:

Mother: 'Your meal is served. You're still watching TV? (enters bed room and switches TV off.)

Child: 'What nonsense! I'm watching a very exciting show! Why did you do this?'

(The child switches the TV on again)

Your positive style:

Mother: "Now it's dinner time. Get ready, dear! Come on and help me in serving the food."

You may get a response like:

Child: "Mom! Can you wait for some time? This is an exciting scene. I don't want to miss it."

Mother: OK, darling! Inform me when it's over."

Child: "Sure, mom!"

Parents! Your patience transfers on to your child.

Child shouts at food served with vegetables and lentils: "I don't like this stuff. Give me Maggie, chips..."

Mother: "You've to eat green vegetables, otherwise I'm going to complain to your father.'

Child: "Do so! I don't care!"

The desirable way is:

Mother: You're big enough to understand the value of vitamins and minerals...without them we'll suffer from many diseases. So, one should have proper food. Listen, darling! Very few people like it, even I don't relish it. But fast food or snacks do more harm than good. Isn't it better for us to have fast food only once in a while?'

Your child may approve of your logical suggestion, and question you like this: "So nice of you, mom!! When will we have that?"

Mother: 'What about having it every weekend?'

The child looks satisfied.

Parents! Try to give some knowledgeable information regarding the value of food. Remember it! That way you are educating your child with vital inputs.

If your daughter is too obsessive about a trendy but daring dress:

Mother: 'I can't allow you to wear such a dress. How do you girls think of exposing yourselves so much? Damn it!'

Child: 'Do you want to make me a laughing stock? I'm not going to hear your conservative talk. Leave me alone! Let me dress in my own way…"

Try this method:

Mother: You look good in this dress…but what about this one? Sometimes dress yourself in a traditional manner…it makes you more glamorous and elegant. Moreover, you'll look different in the group.

Child: Mom! It doesn't look so trendy…Are you serious, Mom! Will I look different?

This type of conversation attracts your child towards you. It suggests that your approach is amenable and your daughter trusts you. This is called "EMOTIONAL BONDING."

If your son/daughter comes with friends of the opposite sex:

Mother: I've given you enough freedom. It doesn't mean you should hang around with these stupid friends.

Child: Mind your language… (He /She may try to break something to show his/her displeasure)

The problem starts right from here. Your child understands your intentions which do not suit his/her mentality and makes a plan to escape…starts telling lots of lies…

The distance between your child and you would not have formed if you had talked to him/her:

Mother: Is she X [her name]? You were talking about her? Hi! Good to see you…"

Parents! Even if you do not appreciate your child's friendship with the opposite sex, you have to accept it initially. Otherwise, you are going to lose future opportunities to help or guide your child in the right direction because they will learn to hide such things from you right from the beginning. That is where the problem starts.

If you find your child busy with the mobile most of the time:

Mother: "I know to whom you're talking. You're wasting both money and time . I warn you if you continue this, be prepared for the consequences…"

Child: Who cares? You'll snatch my mobile…do so…" He retorts at once.

Instead, how about this?

Mother: "Oh! You're still on the phone?... I wanted to talk to you. When you finish speaking, tell me so that I can spend some time with you."

You may expect the following kind of answer:

Child: "Sure, mum, I'll come to you soon."

This kind of conversation sounds healthy and gives you an opportunity to know more about your child, and your child may feel comfortable and secure in revealing the secrets.

Some more examples:

Father, "What nonsense! whenever I am home, I find you stuck to the internet. Now, I warn you I'm going to disconnect the connection."

His teenaged Son stampped his feet, pushed the computer button harshly & went to the bed, pretending he's sleeping.

The Right Way

Father, "Hi Sunny! Give some of your time to me too ..." or "I need your help in searching ... on Google ..."

This is a "positive participation", & your communication skill brings you closer to your son. Because these days "sons" wants to avoid their "Dads" due to their non stop preachings, harsh voice & negative communication.

Father! Catch your son softly!

Father, "Your driving is horrible. I don't understand how you guys're copying the movie-style? If you continue so, I will deprive you from driving a car."

Son looked at him bitterly. He stopped talking to his father at all.

The Right Way

Father, "I know, harsh driving gives an immence pleasure. But this is just a momentary pleasure. Don't you think that many times the momentary pleasures lead us to a permanent destruction? Moreover, your life is so precious for us that I can't even imagine if anything happens untoward!!

Father! Your expression of love definitely shows your mild "objection".

Father is yelling at his son on his reckless expenditure, "This is ridiculous! This is not your fault, it's your mum who is pampering you. Do you've any idea how to make money...?

The Right Way

Father, "Son keep a notebook with you, (you provide him notebook) try to write the expenditures, household to personal, (you may include your expenditure too)."

This is an opening of financial-communication. Your son is certainly learning the usage & value of money. Adopt this method soon, before he becomes the victim of extravagance.

Mother caught her 10 years old daughter, "Oh my God! You are watching adult movie? I always suspect that your friends are not good. This is your study age & you're ruining your future?

The Right Way

"I guess, this kind of movies are made to make money. You know, they show nude pictures just to benefit themselves. They have no moral values and responsibility towards society."

Mother, this is a discussion. Discourage her by being more realistic.

At the same time you're removing her fear & guilt.

Why does a child spend much of their time on the Internet, Facebook or the mobile?

1. They often lack other sources of entertainment;
2. They fulfil their curiosity through the Net in the absence of proper relationship with their parents;
3. Many parents claim to be friendly with their children but they do not know that they preach a lot so their children take it that the parents are against them, which made them keep themselves at a distance from their parents. So, parents! Listen more and talk less. Remember that a child's perception is quite different from that of their parents. Find out the gaps.

Your teenage child comes back from the party in a drunken state:

Mother: (with shouts and cries and almost hysterical) I know you're following your father's footsteps! It's disgusting to see you in such a deplorable state. (In some cases, mother reacts) Get out! How dare you come home like this! Don't you see that I've fights with your father every night only on this issue?... I really hate you...."

Dear mother!

Why can't you act in the following manner if your child has just started taking alcohol?

Mother: "Oh, you're back? You've taken alcohol? I find that you're not able to take care of yourself. Let me help you."

At the very first moment, you showed NO NEGATIVE reactions over his indulgence because you comprehended the delicate situation. Once you sniffed out the predicament you have to keep cool and be patient.

Find a suitable time and talk to your child soberly about the drinking, the party and other addictions. The circumstances and the manner of coping with them can make or mar career issues through the nature of discussions. Eighteen and under is an extremely sensitive age group. Moreover, if you find that his father is an alcoholic, instead of abusing his father why don't you talk to your child in the following manner:

Look, dear, your father has an addiction and you often disapproved of it. You know addiction is a sort of disease, and once you're under the influence of drug or alcohol, people will start cheating and duping you, making a fool of you, and even try to take advantage of your weakness which is plainly visible to your competitors or enemies; and you will also fail to identify difficult situations when you are under the extraneous influence. There are ample numbers of examples which cite how people lost money and reputation due to the small cravings which led them along a path where nothing exists except failures or misery. The effect of alcohol is so strong that often you lose even your own identity because it affects your brain. You've to perform many deeds in your life. How can you make yourself worthy if you continue like this? You must think on these lines. Better nip your bad habit in the bud.

Mother! You have sent the correct and timely message to your child. You can educate them by discussing and searching for the effects of alcohol on the brain and other parts of the body, e.g. liver, through Internet. A child, too, learns to utilise the Internet services.

Lots of adults accuse their parents for their alcoholism because they often used to condemn their habit of alcohol when they started it (the average age of onset is generally sixteen or earlier), which made them more adamant and rigid. They regretted that if their parents had been friendly and been guiding them properly their future would not have been dark and aimless.

Talk with your teenage child about his career goals. Participate actively in such discussions. Divert his mind from life of ease and ostentation not only by delivering lectures but by searching for information and prospects through surfing the Net and discussing about the future and careers without making a fuss over it. You have to go ahead to fix him in a suitable career. Do not limit yourself here but talk to him often about his subjects and likings by involving yourselves actively. You can see the difference.

When your child approaches eighteen, your role will be absolutely different. If you worked hard up to eighteen years of your child in a positive and fruitful manner, stop worrying about him much.

❑❑❑

Challenging Parenting

Working Mother

The worst affected mothers in the globe are working mothers. Their guilt feelings and confused state of mind make matters worse. However, in the changing world, especially in India, the meaning of 'mother' is also changing with the new role of modern and working mothers.

It is a pleasant surprise to find that a good number of children feel proud to have working mothers. These days, children of mothers who stay indoors have a kind of inferiority complex. The problem with the working mother is related to the lack of management. Management springs from one's disciplined and skilled quality of leadership. When you are responsible for meeting both ends, you will have to be pleasant and charming inwardly and outwardly. Working women! The first thing people notice about you is your facial expression which is your basic asset. Working mothers often suffer from a feeling of inadequacy as they feel themselves incapable of balancing their two roles. Their frustration which comes out in the form of anger or depression snatches every moment from them. Every moment has its own value and significance, especially for the working woman. Respect your moments. A mother was suffering from a guilt feeling that she is doing injustice to her six-year-old child because when he comes from school he does not find his mother. Yes, this is a hard time, of course; but you have to discover how to provide emotional attachment even when you are away.

Never forget to keep a chit written, "Enjoy your meal. Love you, I'm missing you", close to the dining table, plate or any noticeable place.

These words have tremendous encouraging power which certainly help the child grow with a positive frame of mind. Never waste your time in throwing tantrums.

Evening tea and dinner should be arranged in such a way that you should have them with your child. Many mothers tend to put their children to bed because they have to go to school early in the morning and engaging in such act unnecessarily takes time because everyone sleeps according to one's own pattern. So it is better to have dinner together and sleep at the same hours.

SINGLE PARENT

It becomes difficult when one has to take charge of single parenthood. The latter may be the result of death of the spouse, divorce or separation. Whatever may be the reason, the responsibility and the challenge are the same. But sometimes the background also matters and needs careful and soft handling by taking into account the sensitivity of the situation.

The death of a parent is a sensitive issue. The effects of death can be devastating for a child.

The death of the mother in particular shatters a child's world and it becomes hard for them to collect himself/themselves emotionally, for it leaves a vacuum in their lives. In such cases, a father becomes helpless in handling or taking care of his child's emotional needs, whereas the death of the father puts a child in a totally different position as their social status may change in a day. Their life just goes in reverse. The physical and financial protection and security gets a jolt at an early stage of a child's life which makes them vulnerable to any kind of stress. The mother finds herself lost and confused regarding fulfillment of her child's needs and multiple tasks outside and inside. Divorce on the other hand may be a mutual and planned separation, but still a child needs both parents for his mental and physical well-being. However, in any form, single parenthood entails a life of onerous responsibility which calls for careful handling of one's child.

SINGLE MOTHER

A bereaved wife soon prepares to take charge of all the important spheres of life when she is alone with her kids and seeks ways to meet the needs and demands of her children. In India, the joint family is breaking up rapidly and under such circumstances there is no choice for a mother but to collect herself and accept the facts and the challenges of life without succumbing to the crisis.

"I never had a thought of this kind...I couldn't even cry on my husband's death...because I was surrounded by my two kids, aged seven and ten...my children had no concept of death...I realised that my battle had begun which certainly won't end in defeat or victory on my selfish part...but as a mother with kids I'd my own duty towards my children." Anima's life had turned upside down and she was sobbing between the words. "I try to keep myself calm. My son who is now twelve and daughter who is fifteen show absolutely opposite kinds of behaviour. However, they used to ask me about their dad every now and then. I tried to manage by showing lots of similar instances but I think that things are now quite different with the passage of time. My son is becoming aggressive and lies a lot whereas my daughter keeps silent most of the time. My son has lots of friends, whereas my daughter does not make friends with anyone. This contrasting behaviour makes me frustrated; so as a result, I, too, can't control myself and become impatient quite often. I don't know how, after putting in so much effort, it has borne no fruits."

There are several Animas who are encountering similar situations. The loss of the loved one is irreparable and irreversible. This could be the saddest part of one's family history. However, such accidents do happen at times.

Anima tried to parent her children in a good way with a good motive as much as she could. But the problem with her was that her own issues at times overpowered her and then her growing children could not comprehend the normal problems of their mother due to their immaturity. However, on the mother's part, too, a sort of immaturity may be evident due to her single parenthood. She might not be adept in handling the issues at which the male is supposed to be more efficient. Hence, uncertainty and fears may pave the way for anxiety, depression and anger in her, which are related to the propensity to use immature coping mechanisms like indecisiveness, self-blame, hostile reaction and submissiveness. The poor coping style in the mother due to her high anxiety disposition, perhaps her worry about other people making opinion/comments on her, is a major motivator in her life that could make her defensive and guarded. As a result, she is unable to adjust to the circumstances properly and with dignity. Anima was answering my questions firmly and maturely:

"Yes! I had to take the help of other people to motivate me…I didn't take the help of my relatives because of my self-respect…I know, relatives' small favours will not be projected in the proper perspective which is certainly not acceptable to me or my children in the long run… I'm looking after my husband's business where I come across lots of people…a single woman's job is tougher…she becomes the target of people perhaps waiting to exploit…I'm waiting for my children to grow up…'

On the part of her children, her son reported, "My mom doesn't allow me to watch television…she doesn't like it if I talk to my friends over the phone…she doesn't allow me to attend birthday parties of my friends… she even refuses to give me pocket-money…she always wants to see me with my text books…"

Anima's daughter reported, "I'm very depressed to see my mom's onerous responsibilities. I'm unable to share my feelings and problems with her as it may double her problems…people talk against my mom and sometimes they talk about my mom's character, too. I'm very confounded. I don't want to talk to anyone. My brother is younger than me and he lies a lot because he tries to make mom happy. The problem with my mother is that she herself is so much perturbed due to all these responsibilities plus liabilities that I don't want to share my problems with her. It may increase her stress-level so I prefer to stay quiet."

The weakness of the mother's personality is often perceived by her children extremely negatively so that her intentions to bring up her children properly are thwarted. Anima, even putting her entire efforts into it, could not parent her children in the right direction. Her "efforts" and "she-herself" might not be seen by her children separately. In fact, a child wants to see their parents happy and enthusiastic. But a single mother may not come up to the expectation of her child on such delicate issues. A mother who is a single parent should adhere to the following rules:-

1. Make your child aware of the fact that without a father the life may be somewhat different but not a miserable one. Accept it. You may give some realistic and positive examples of others who have gone through such a crisis.
2. Being a single mother, you should prepare yourself as a person with the right emotional quotient because you are not the single case of this kind.
3. You have to fulfil your child's needs and desires which were supposed to be the dad's responsibility, like helping and encouraging him to form his ideas related to business and money matters. Discuss with

him your business or job-related hindrances and seek some advice from him. Discussing about business or work does not mean that you have to go according to his suggestions but this might boost his self-confidence. A child may feel wanted and have a feeling of their own existence. In this way, they will be more cooperative and less complaining.

4. Be more gentle. The outer and the inner activities are two opposite poles. Play the role of Libra—make them equal and balanced. Show your efficiency in the outer world and at the same time be a good homemaker. Many working women lack this quality. You might observe that you waste your time on unnecessary arguments, complaining about your children, spouse (even after death!), members of the family or even your cooks and assistants. By doing this, you spoil your precious mood and zeal, out of your own irritability. Thus valuable time slips from you and you end up exhausting yourself. Your child needs you with your cool and enthusiastic temperament. It is a positive tool which helps in filling the vacuum through which your child is going through in your absence. Fill it with your smile, songs, chirpiness and other good and pleasant activities.
5. If you try to compensate your absence only with objects, you are certainly accumulating and inviting more problems and preparing a dangerous future for your child. Because emotional deprivation is a big setback which is only cured or filled by emotional reciprocation.
6. If you leave for your workplace and come back after your child is back from school, do not forget to leave a chit with words such as "Relish your lunch…love, mom." It is a way to fill your absence with abstract feelings in your child. And your child will understand you more.
7. It is advisable for a single parent to find a trustworthy friend with whom she feels free to vent her emotional feelings. You do not need to talk much about that person because your child may have a feeling that your attention is being shared by an outsider.
8. If he is a man and you are ready for a permanent liaison with him, wait for some time. Find a suitable time to talk to your child and share your difficulties of being alone. Leave the decision to them for the time being. You should keep silent for a considerable period of

time. You will certainly get a favourable answer from your child. It is applicable when your child is grown up. If your child is still small, take the help of a professional, instead of relatives or friends, who can talk to the child logically and convincingly.

SINGLE FATHER

Many cases of a single father revealed that the father is entirely inefficient in managing his kids. His inefficiency revolves around either his own adamant behaviour, ill-temperament or leniency/laxity. These too extreme temperaments of the father stand as obstacles in the progression of his child. A motherless child finds himself inept in sending messages to their father, especially in the Indian set-up, where child rearing is considered to be the mother's zone. It is seen that most children use their mother as an intermediary if they want something from their father, so mothers become a go-between in the child-father relationship. Loss of the mother becomes critical for a child, and the father himself is often helpless in controlling and parenting his child. A father should understand the nuances of parenting. The following tips may work for a single father:

1. Taking physical care may be translated into emotional support. Most of the time a father is a failure in maintaining a child in both respects. So it is advisable for him to perform a few practical tasks with lots of emotional ingredients. The latter include encouragement, praise, rewards (besides hugging, kissing or any form of affectionate touch). Because one can perhaps find a physical provider but not an emotional supporter.
2. He should trust his child and mix with his friends and their parents. He should not miss parent–teacher meetings, the sports day or any event in his child's school.
3. He should take care of the child's homework and experiences in school and discuss with his peers or teachers on a regular basis.
4. He should not forget to celebrate the child's birthday and invite their friends.
5. He should celebrate festivals in the child's company, and never miss giving gifts or new clothes on these occasions.
6. The father should jointly do routine activities, like brushing of teeth, morning walk, yoga, or any kind of exercise, and also

perhaps prepare some dishes—sometimes according to the child's choices and sometimes those of his own. In this way, the child may regularize their daily activities and forget the trauma of being alone. Slowly they will master such situations. In this way, a father may come out of the trauma of this big loss as well.

7. Washing clothes, cleaning and decorating the home with the father may work as a panacea.
8. Fulfilling every desire of the child may be detrimental to their wellness because they might begin to take it for granted and when the father is unable to fulfill his (child's) wishes he (the child) may not be comfortable in such situations. So one should avoid being over-protective and submissive too often.
9. A father can prove himself a good parent if he works a little more and think sensibly.

DIVORCED PARENTS

Many single parents rush to my clinic or to me seeking advice and suggestions in shock and terror, being helpless and having failed at parenting in two diametrically opposite ways.

"I'm a single mom and life is so much tough for me now. I do not have confidence that what I'm doing is right for my son. I am afraid to take my son out in public because of the scenes he creates. If he wants to take anything he becomes obstinate and if I refuse he starts biting, hitting, kicking and even rolling on the ground to have it. His aggression and incessant whining are out of control."

A child of divorced parent needs considerable emotional support. First of all, he has already been tortured by the active or cold war between the parents which may have left a big scar on his mind. Watching parental discord is in itself an emotional jolt and parting with one parent is like the death of one's natural desires, feelings and security. Especially in the Indian set-up where divorce is still not too common, it fills a child with fears, insecurity and, inferiority complex and as a result, he easily becomes the victim of social anxiety and face lots of social stigma for being a child of divorced parents. However, under such circumstances, parents should take extra care of their child's well-being. When divorce is inevitable, parents should make sure not to poison their child's mind with their bitterness towards the other parent. Because a child never accepts the faults when presented by one parent, in order to save himself or herself. Your child cannot be judgmental on such a delicate issue. His love for both the parents is unbiased and indivisible. He often loves his mother as much as his father. So there is no point in recounting the mistakes of your spouse before your child. The problem is that the perception of a normal family is usually considered to be structured by two parents. However, there are a large number of parents who are single. A single parent's first duty is to create a positive and pleasant environment for their child.

1. The life of a single parent may be hectic and busy. It is difficult to give your child all your time. The following tips may be beneficial for single parents:
2. Keep in touch with family and friends so that when you need their help, say, in a crisis, they will extend a helping hand.
3. Please them constantly by dropping in at their place with lots of gifts, sweets and any other material stuff. So that you can feel your child and yourself wanted.
4. If they have children, try to shower your love and affection on them, too.
5. Always appreciate them, their home decoration and cooking, and if possible please them by extending your helping hand by doing some domestic chores, like helping in cooking, dish washing, cleaning etc..
6. Avoid being an unwanted guest.
7. It is advisable for you to engage your child in some sort of art or creativity. This can give your child an opportunity to make friends, mix with them and have fun. Moreover, creative thinking and activities may reduce their loneliness and give them energy to overpower life's adversities that arise from being a child in a single-parent family. It will have a positive effect during their socialization period and provide them encouragement and help in becoming a stable and mature person in adulthood.
8. Apart from this, your personal presence will give them confidence to go ahead in life. So, keep some time exclusively for your child at least once in a fortnight and go out and have fun together.

9. Reading the newspaper and magazines, including pages with puzzles, jumbles and scrabbles, brings lots of positive effect in a child's personality. Sharing the news and solving jumbles together in the morning could open the key to success. Never deprive them of this fun which may ultimately change into a good cultured routine and make them more disciplined and educated in the long run.
10. It is normal for parents to get angry and frustrated at times. But do not take out your negative feelings on your child. However, if it happens, keep cool and talk to him: it was not the child who disturbed you but your bad mood which compelled you to lose your temper. The understanding between them as a child and you as a parent is imperative. Your child will certainly understand your anger. "Sorry" may not be the right word to accept one's fault; it is better to clarify the reason for your anger which is necessary to strengthen such an important relationship.
11. It is a delicate time for your child when they have to meet the other parent (legal duration). Never poison his mind by saying anything against the absentee parent involved in legal separation. If possible, try to say something good about your spouse and teach them to behave well with the parent. That will work as a magic potion. If you are jealous and bear a grudge or bitterness against your spouse, better bury the hatchet, because your hatred may transfer to your child's mind, making them weak and confused which would culminate in poor self-esteem or other negative behaviour. So mark the meeting period with their parent as an auspicious day and encourage them to visit him/her with zeal. When he comes back, do not ask many questions about your divorcee spouse because it may spoil your mood but you must ask something on the lines of, "Hope you have enjoyed a lot....". This will be a good gesture and also show your positive concern about your ex-spouse, too. After all, she/he is the parent of your child and she/he cannot be a creature of the past for your child. Take care of it. You may find a dramatic difference in your child's behaviour.
12. There are scores of single parents who struggle needlessly to get their child's cooperation and attention, as they have no clue how their nagging and negative efforts make their child more disobedient and adamant.

JOINT/EXTENDED FAMILY

In such families, either parent may find himself/herself overburdened or relieved. It is again one's personality traits which determine one's behaviour towards the members of the family. One person may consider the joint family as a 'support-system' whereas another may believe it to be a 'curse' in India where the joint family system still prevails to some extent. Parents should keep in mind that their child's socialization could be proper in the joint family where lots of sharing and caring activities take place unitedly. In such families, parenting may not be limited to only the mother and father but may also extend to other senior members of the family. So everyone should have an optimal level of awareness. Since your child is going through the socialization process, you have to be tactful. As a member of a joint family, it demands lots out of you and you have to obey the rules for the sake of the child's personality development. One thing that is important for parents is that, even in a joint family, their child has a third eye (keen perception) which only revolves around their parents' behaviour, nullifying the effects of the negative behaviour of other members of the family. Remember, your child keenly perceives you as a parent as well as a person. Other members of the family are not too important in this context if you are competent enough. This means, if parents provide a good training to their child, the latter has an ability to avoid other related factors, like, punishment/rejection received from their grandparents, say. Thus the responsibility of good parenting, in a joint family, rests a great deal with the parents. Their excuses, if they fail to administer a good parenting style for their children, show their own anguish or helplessness vis-à-vis the other members of the family.

SIBLING RIVALRY

The term 'sibling rivalry' means the jealousy, negative competition and even the fighting between the brothers and sisters.

Why does this occur?

Generally, sibling rivalry is strong when a new baby arrives. The shift of love and care of the parents from the elder to the younger is very common. However, parents also take a note and are often cautious about their elder child's care and activities. Still they fail to resolve the conflicts between their children. As a matter of fact, parents have some pre-notion that the elder child should understand that the younger one is helpless because he does not speak or perform any activities on his own. So, the parents have to help and take care of the younger one more frequently than the elder one. They often utter, rebuke or scold the elder one that he should understand this predicament and compel him to behave according to their instructions. The problem starts right from here which may continue till adulthood if the conflict is not resolved in early childhood.

"I'm so much exhausted while I see my both children are fighting like a cat and dog. I'm developing migraine. I guess it may be due to their uncontrollable behaviour. I'm perplexed how to react in such circumstances? My elder son often copies my younger son. Even when he was six months old, he used to behave as if he too is six months old child. Please help." Sukanta, mother of two children, aged two years and eight years respectively, was sitting in front of me with a haggard face.

The elder child watches his parents minutely and, at the same time, notes/observes how his younger sibling is behaving, which makes his parents prompt in attending him. In some extreme cases, the elder one starts bed-wetting after seeing his sibling doing so.

How to resolve this conflict?

Parents! The best way to resolve the forthcoming conflict is to talk to your elder child sensibly before the arrival of a new baby.

The following is the sample list: "Look baby! A new baby is coming. So, our first duty is to look after him because when he will be born, he cannot speak or express his problems. So, we have to see his problems. And a new baby is born without teeth. So I will have to feed him.....You have to do this work and I'll do that work. When he'll grow up, he'll be your best brother/sister and friend."

Such kind of conversation may relax a child and, having this feedback, he may assist you rather than comparing himself with a new one.

Twinkle, an eight-year-old-girl, was looking tense. In her own words: "My mom and dad often kiss my brother Sanchay (nine months old male baby). They used to kiss me and hug me when he was not born.

Now they often scold me if I try to touch him. They frequently say that I should take care of my little brother. They gave me a separate bed now for sleeping because Sanchu has to sleep where I used to. I feel that they've stopped loving me now."

The parents' reaction: "Twinkle is now grown up. We make her understand that she is no more a baby. So, she should behave like an elder sister. We still love her very much but she often thinks that I'm being partial. However, Sanchu is small and needs lots of care. But she is not able to understand this. She makes lots of noises very often. Her tantrums are unbearable."

There was a family of four with two sons that came to me in groups

Ravi was accompanied by his father whose complaint was that this son of his was getting introverted by the day, and so he was unsure of what he would do in life? The father was also puzzled by the fact that his mother didn't quite see anything remarkable in the child's attitude.

True to his father's word, Ravi came out as a shy individual who didn't make any eye-contact with me.

On the other hand, Sunny felt unloved in the absence of his father.

He was introduced by his mother as a bit rebellious, who would not comply with any requirement, unlike Ravi. Her other complaint was that Sunny would often provoke Ravi to such an extent that Ravi would be forced to react. The brothers, therefore, had frequent quarrels. His father though didn't think that Sunny was rebellious. He felt that one should be outgoing and this attitude would help Sunny in later life.

On careful consideration, what came out was a stark analysis that resides in numerous homes even as you read this. There appeared to me a clear inclination of the father and mother towards Sunny and Ravi respectively. This had maybe unintentionally brought in a feeling of bitterness in the brothers. This, in turn, had led to sibling rivalry with lots of quarrels daily adding to the effect. Parents innocently sow the seeds of rivalries and jealousy in their children. Their own unintentional favouritism may create problems and build a wall between the siblings.

This needs to be looked at closely. Parents must realise that bias towards either child, for whatever reason, only serves to drive a wedge between the children. Parents need to try and connect with all their children and to paint them with the same brush ubiquitously when it comes to love and affection. They also need to try and do everything as a family, with all children involved, so that nobody feels left out to any extent. This leads to a strong family bonding, and lays a firm foundation for sibling closeness.

❑❑❑

PART-IV

OOPS! SEX!

Sex: Let's Face The Truth

In today's society, teenagers are becoming more and more involved in sexual relationships. Many parents are confused about how to talk to their child about sexual matters. In fact, India is so conservative on such issues that talking about sex with their own teens is largely still taboo—even for the open-minded parents.

However, several parents are gradually accepting that sex education should begin at home—but they are at a loss to decide how to start. It needs to be imparted by parents, and teenagers should learn about the outcome of a sexual relationship. Teenaged pregnancy is on the rise in India, and so, too, the number of abortions. The best way to prevent a teenager from accidental and unwanted pregnancies is, for parents, especially mothers, to come forward and get involved in their child's activities and lifestyle as a friend and as a guide.

Sex is a normal urge so parents should not get embarrassed on this issue. Indian parents forget that the guru of sex was Indian and that sex has a big role in ancient paintings and sculptures of India. They overlook this when they go off with their children to visit the renowned temples and caves; for example, Khajuraho, Konarak etc., where the depiction of sex in art is the first aspect which is noticed and for which they are famous, and people from all over the world go there to capture their beauty. So, parents! Why be ashamed or strict while dealing with such issues with your child? Is it not something which shows your duality? Sex is a not a subject to be taught. Can we teach our children to perform their bodily functions? But the problem is that it is something which is directly related to a pleasurable sensation. And this sensation is related to one's glands and hormones, which is why it is considered as a biological urge.

Sex is an essential urge. When a person is fully grown and all the hormones of the body start functioning normally, they have a different kind of feeling. This feeling can be controlled. It is not at all involuntary like other bodily functions.

Words like 'sex is dirty' or 'it is a sin' may induce sexual aversion and fears in one's life and may make one's adult and sexual life miserable—and those words are not in keeping with practice.

I have come across many adolescents who suffer from masturbation-guilt and, as a result, they usually become the victims of anxiety and depression. They do not have sound sleep, boys suffer from nocturnal emission, and even girls of this age have a tremendous guilt feeling because of the lack of proper knowledge and guidance. They consider masturbation a crime and do not want to face anyone, but most of the time they spend daydreaming or imagining about sex. Parents' own biases on such a delicate issue fill them with fears and insecurity and turn them into a constant and vigilant guard of their children. They seem terribly upset and puzzled in handling these natural and normal problems of their children, particularly if they find out any trace of sexual involvement of their child, like porn magazines or CDs, condoms and birth control pills.

It is observed through a large number of case histories that parents become whimsical and start reacting in a very inappropriate manner even with their grown-up child by asking , "Who gives you such dirty CDs …Oh! I know about those friends of yours, those who often indulge in such dirty activities, stop meeting them, form a group of good friends, otherwise stay alone…this is your career making time. You can't involve yourself in all this indecent stuff. Stay away from all this stuff…"

These kinds of parental reactions go towards making the child either aggressive or depressive. It depends on the temperament of the victim (child), who becomes confused in the absence of a good guide who could show him the right direction.

Parents! You have to be very careful while handling such delicate issues. Your child wants you to be honest and most of the time he counts on you. So your improper reactions and advice may make him vulnerable to any stress and, as a sequel to this, he may be prone to commit mistakes irrespective of social values and norms, like teenage pregnancy, sexually transmitted diseases, abortion and other sexual aberrations.

- Sex is indispensable. Accept it. So while interacting with your child listen to him as much as possible without interruptions. After hearing his point of view about sex, you may add more information without sounding like preaching to him.
- Do not react if he recounts his experiences before you. Your reaction may be an indication that you are discouraging him and he may soon lose his interest in revealing himself.

- If he has committed any mistakes listen patiently to the incidents. Do not let him feel disheartened.
- Masturbation is a common practice. Do not fill him with the ideas that it is something shameful. But excessive masturbation may cause some psychological problems, so encourage him to do some creative work, develop a hobby and/or perform physical activity, such as, swimming, cycling or running, or join a sports club. In this way he can burn his energy which is essential for sound health, and psychologically as well. This is the right way to curb his excessive sexual desire.
- Be direct and honest. Do not give him any false information if you feel it is "dirty". Sex in itself is not dirty, but false perception of sex is dirty. Accurate information of sex consists of many aspects, like, social values, maturity in action, emotional involvement, sensitivity, and potential risks. Be careful your talks should be absolutely as a guide and not as a preacher; otherwise your child will not take you seriously and feel, "She/he is too preachy!" And he will soon stop opening up to you.
- The child will listen when you talk to him in a simple manner. Do not bombard him with too much information at a time. Do your part as a parent and raise him with the proper information at a proper age that could save him from many problems. Step-by-step information may make his life healthier and he will take it rationally.
- Remember, while talking to him that your child should not be just a passive listener. Encourage him to put some questions and show curiosity. If he keeps silent, it means you are just wasting your time. So make it a two-way communication.

Apart from that, childhood sexual curiosity is a most common phenomenon.

Arpita was looking terrified and unable to comprehend the behaviour of her seven-year-old daughter who has formed a habit of playing with her genitals whenever she is alone. Such a case is not rare. I had to pacify her by explaining and informing about this normal behaviour of a child in the following manner:

"Sex drive has a hormonal base but stimulation of the genitals is innately pleasurable so sex is not related or restricted only to hormonal development and a small child, too, starts experimenting. This pleasure may be stimulated by discovering or exploring the pleasure zone of the body. This kind of sensation may be derived from a tender age when a small child explores the genital region suddenly and finds a pleasurable sensation. This may be a sheer pleasure which may well go away over time."

But parents who see this action on a bigger canvas and react inappropriately suddenly trigger their child's interest or fear in this field unintentionally by being more vigilant towards her.

Vani, the mother of a six-year-old daughter was looking tense because she saw her daughter's cousin brother, who was almost of the same age, kissing her daughter.

I told Vani, "Sometimes we need to ignore it as 'child's play'—actually it is a common practice and usually indulged in by groups of children from their infancy. So parents should not be getting too worried about such actions of their child. It is a brief game where the child wants to play the role of senior members of the house. But parents should not leave their child unattended to and are advised to intervene carefully. They should also be cautions because during sleeping hours (nights) many a child wakes up and may see parental intimate relationship. Sometimes a child gets terrified too and sometimes he also tries to practise the same."

INNOCENT VICTIM

A number of problems, like vomiting, headache, stomach ache, anxiety, and fears are common in a child and they have the root cause in a child's molestation, as observed during the interview session. An infant from just after birth till twelve years of age sorely needs physical protection. The immature child has no idea of molestation or rape. Sexual abuse is common in the Indian set-up and the child becomes the easy victim where close family members or outsiders may take advantage of a child's ignorance and innocence. Most cases of obsession and adjustment disorder in parents have an underlying history of their own sexual abuse in their childhood which made them indifferent and apathetic towards the most demanding situations, like self-care and child-rearing practice.

Touch: To save the child from being the victim of sexual abuse, it is the mother who should teach the child and make them aware of the "feeling of touch" and 'intention of touch". It is a delicate issue but telling your child about his/her sexuality and training them on how to prevent this kind of thing happening, although seemingly difficult, yet can save your child from a traumatic future.

HOW: You have to make your child aware of his/her private parts of the body and talk in a simple but convincing way: "Look! Sometimes elderly and experienced persons are prone to touch the private parts of your body because they take you as an innocent child. And if you do not raise your voice out of fear they may take the next step and may do you harm. So just be careful. If you find someone is bothering you in this way you must raise an alarm to prevent the next step from happening and immediately inform your parents. Don't get scared if the particular person threatens you."

Sex education should be provided by parents as soon as possible because a child's natural curiosity is aroused when they start thinking. The best way to provide sex education is by talking to them about the reproductive systems of plants followed by animals which is a part of the curriculum in the primary section in schools. When a child comes to know about the reproductive system in plants and animals, parents should start by degrees with the reproductive system in human beings. A better way to make the child understand is to draw a picture of the human anatomy and then reply to some of the questions triggered off by their curiosity by explaining them systematically and methodically. You can apply this method to small children, too. The benefit of this education is that you do not feel embarrassed when such situations occur, as when you are watching a movie together or having magazines in your home, or sometimes they catch sight of, or catch rapping, you in your bed with your spouse.

"A husband was making love to his wife, his eight-year-old child suddenly entered his parents' bed room and looked frightened and shocked; his parents took the right step, quickly managed themselves and told him, "Come on, son! When did you wake up?" They started common and easy conversation.

Suppose if the reaction to their son's sudden entry was, "Go away!... go!... can't you knock on the door? Don't you have any manners?"

However, when a child asks about your intimate relations you can answer him confidently that, "Look we are your parents so we love each other very much". It solely depends on you how you deliver such information without elaborating and exaggerating.

Observe the distinct reactions of the parents. The first reaction is assuring your child and educating him as well, which has a positive impact on his life in the long run. The second reaction may fill their child with guilt, anxiety, shame, fear and confusion which has a bad impact on his general mental state and may result in poor concentration and poor sexual life in his later years.

The second benefit is that your child will never feel ashamed if he wants to know anything about sex. It will open a door for every communication between your child and you.

Most importantly, your child would hardly commit any sex-related crime. He may feel secure by finding such good parents in the form of friends and guides.

Sometimes we have to quarrel for setting matters concerning the family life, and, on other occasions, we have to increase our intimacy with each other through the art of love. It is analogous to the situation where we are constrained to scold our child and, when occasion demands, we are also privileged to fondle the child.

"Mom! Why do dad and you sleep together?" This might be a common question raised by almost every little child. The worried parents fail to reply in a proper manner, muttering, "When you grow up you'll understand!...

The duty of parents is to satisfy the curiosity of their child by answering him properly and without lying: "Look! This is the custom. Your father and I are a family. So we should stay together as much as possible." This is a simple and satisfying answer for a child aged three years onwards.

SAVE YOUR CHILD FROM SEXUAL EXPLOITATION

It is very sad that children are sometimes exploited sexually by known or unknown persons who often have our confidence and trust. These people spend considerable time in targeting and establishing trust to gain access to a child. Sexual abuse can be physical, verbal or emotional; and can cause physical and emotional harm to a child. A number of suicidal tendencies and maladjustments in later life, can also be linked to the childhood trauma and sexual exploitation. In few cases, an exploited child might turn into an antisocial element. The child may become indifferent towards the sensitive issues of the society. He/she might assume that rape is a normal phenomenon because his/her own exploiters seldom got punished.

Sexual abuse does not mean just rape. It could be present in different forms and may include the following:

• kissing or holding a child in a sexual manner • exposing a sexual body part to a child • having sexual relations with a child • talking in a sexually explicit way that is not age or developmentally appropriate • making obscene phone calls or remarks to a child • sending obscene mobile text messages or emails to a child • fondling a child in a sexual manner • persistently intruding on a child's privacy • penetrating the child's vagina or anus by either the penis, finger or any other object • exposing their genitals to a child • oral sex • rape • incest • showing pornographic films, magazines, internet sites or photographs to a child • having a child pose or perform in a sexual manner • forcing a child to watch a sexual act etc.

An abused child usually says or does things or exhibit certain physical signs that may indicate sexual abuse. Most often, because of fear, anxiety and ignorance he/she does not give the complete details of the incident. We,being parents, should always be on our guard. But we, being busy with our daily routines, and also not sufficiently prepared for these kinds of incidents and situations, often miss these subtle hints and signs. Rather, we often scold or ignore our children. We generally perceive these hints as lame excuses for their disinterest in studies or refusal to go to school. All these physical complaints may have direct correlation to their psychological and mental state and their abnormal behaviour and deep anxieties. Parents who guide the children appropriately during their sensitive years (4-10) hardly have any emotional-crisis in their later life.

Some indicators of child sexual abuse may include:

• difficulty in concentrating or being withdrawn or overly obedient • having unexpected redness, soreness or injury around the penis, vagina, mouth or anus • having torn, stained or bloody clothing, especially underwear • displaying greater sexual knowledge than normally expected for their age or developmental level • inappropriate sexual play and behaviour with themselves, other children or dolls and toys • hints about sexual activity through actions or comments that are inappropriate to the child's age or developmental level • excessive masturbation or masturbation in public after kindergarten age • persistent bed wetting, urinating or soiling in clothes • persistent sexual themes in their drawings or play time • running away • hurting or mutilating animals • creating stories, poems or artwork about abuse etc.

Should any of the above be present, it is our duty and responsibility as parents to take immediate action to keep our children safe from any further harm.

To protect a child from sexual abuse, we should be wary of people who are overly affectionate or generous with gifts to our child. Always be suspicious if an adult wants to spend time alone with your child or regularly offers to babysit a child for free or take a child on overnight outings alone or actively isolates a child from other adults or children or insists on physical affection such as kissing, hugging, wrestling or tickling even when the child clearly does not want it or enjoys taking lots of pictures of children or shares alcohol or drugs with younger children or adolescents or exposes their genitals to a child, etc.

Teach children that their body parts covered by underwear are private. Encourage them to shout and say 'NO' if anyone tries to touch their private parts.

Talk to children about personal safety rules and how to apply them in potentially dangerous situations in simple language. Often play 'what if' games to reinforce the message.

This is a call for parents to standby their children without fear and stigma. A set of questionnaire is given for the awareness of parents to save their children, and to pre-empt any abuse. (Answer in either Yes or No). Please be honest when you tick your answer.

1. Do you leave your child to the care taker?
2. Does the care-taker look after all the responsibilities of your child (such as toilet training and showering)?
3. Does your child share the bed of care-taker or any other relative?
4. Do you allow your child to undress himself/herself in the presence of other family members before and after taking a bath?
5. Does your child move around the house unclothed?
6. Do you object if anyone kisses or hugs your child out of affection?
7. Do you scold your child when he/she makes any complaint against servants, priests, family friends or relatives?
8. Do you ignore the basic reasons of your child's ailments (vomiting, nausea, headache, stomach-ache etc.)?
9. Do you avoid/scold when your child is curious about sex?
10. Do you think your child is too small to wrap a towel before and after a shower?
11. Do you ignore when someone close to the family makes funny comments while your child wraps the towel around his/her waist?
12. Do you object if someone makes fun of your child's private parts, lowers his/her pants, passes comments or jeers at him/her?
13. Do you leave your child unattended with his/her tutor?

14. Do you believe that a priest, teacher or guru will never harm your child?
15. Do you scold your child when he/she comes to you with complaints of molestation?
16. Are you easily convinced by teachers, priests, gurus or relatives rather than your child?
17. Are you too busy to listen to your child's happenings/activities in the school regularly?
18. Do you avoid your child's stammer and stuttering problem?
19. Do you think it is a wastage of time to talk to your child about school teachers, bus conductors and security persons?
20. Do you think that it is too early to teach a child how to defend himself/herself when someone behaves strangely and sexually?
21. Do you think that a male child does not need to be protected from sexual exploitation?
22. Do you bother if your child looks fearful, stressed and anxious?
23. Does your child fear opening up to you because of your hard attitude?
24. Do you find yourself unable to give priority to your child's everyday activities at home and school after returning from your work?
25. Do you block or avoid your child's expressions by letting them know that you are "worn-out" after coming back from work?
26. Do you often ignore your child's habit of thumb-sucking, bed wetting, etc.?
27. Do you scold your child when he wakes up often in the mid of night?

Note: In case, if any of your answers shows that you have been little careless or ignorant about the disturbed mental status of your child, do not panic. There might be some other reasons associated to his/her manifestation of anxiety. However, do not take the matter lightly. Always listen to your child with trust and faith what they say, even if it shocks you. Children rarely make up stories about sexual abuse. Come closer to your child with affection and love and get to know about the reasons of his stress. Shower your love when she/he confides in you about her/his sex-exploitation. Make sure you stand by your children, and not scold or blame them for the ill-fortunate situation. A confident and loving parent has sufficient ingredients to save their children from becoming the victim of sexual exploitation. Make sure to build a trust and faith between you and your child so that they feel confident of your support and start sharing their problems with you. Parents are the strong pillars where no trespasser dare cross. Make and create a healthy ambiance in and around the family. Let your child grow under your pleasant supervision.

❑❑❑

PART-V

Construction or Destruction?

Academics Related Truth

Some parents put excessive pressure on their children. They expect them to excel in academics as well as in other activities irrespective of the child's abilities. High expectations from your child are good from the development point of view but this expectation should be realistic. Your child's area of interest lies in some particular subject but you are pressurizing him/her to follow a course according to your interest. Here, you have to be very careful.

Today's kindergarten cannot give kids the scope to liberate their mind. A space, where a baby requires to apply his own brain, is now missing. Learning is now a mechanical process.

Academic pressure ends up distorting, and ultimately, destroying the natural mode of learning. Parents believe that their child's learning capacities depend on the effectiveness of coaching centres and private tuitions to provide them with the proper tools to encounter education. Parents! Do you realise that REAL learning does not come from stuffy classrooms and rote education, but is based on the "Trial and Error Method?" Do you realise that education is not something to be fought with or an obstacle to overcome, but the process of true self-reflection and the imbibing of skills and ideas that lead to complete, wholesome growth of the faculties of the mind, body and soul? A child should be encouraged to try and fail, and then to try and fail some more, until he learns to correct his own mistakes. Since time immemorial, man has inescapably relied upon his own instincts of preservation and his own mental faculties to develop mechanisms to cope with the world around him. And to this day, these attributes are very much ingrained in the impressionable mind of our own children. Unless you give your child the scope and space to make his own mistakes and to learn from them, he will never truly appreciate the value of effort. It is most certainly your duty to protect your child from external negativities and irregularities; however, too much protection runs the risk of subduing the full growth and flowering of your child's own defences and inherent talents. Remember the story of the caterpillar, which was freed from its cocoon far too early, and was thus unable to transform into the beautiful butterfly that it was destined to be? Your child is that caterpillar, striving towards the metamorphosis into a complete, well-rounded individual. The role of a parent is to ensure that the cocoon remains unharmed as the caterpillar is growing, and not to cut open the cocoon to try and create short-cuts for his/her children. The child will grow and mature through his own efforts, mistakes and successes. Give your child the freedom to make his own mistakes. Once he has made a mistake, ask him to reflect on where he went wrong, and what steps he could have taken to correct himself. Let him think on his own and judge the situation for himself. Once your child realises that his parents trust him implicitly, he will be further encouraged to test his own boundaries of efforts and achievements, and only then will he be able to truly explore every possibility within himself. Remember: mistakes are not a manifestation of the faults within you, but the endless vista of the hitherto unexplored realities that lie waiting.

In today's world, it has become somewhat of a trend to start children's schooling and education from the very tender age of two. A child starts facing academic and intellectual pressures from the very beginning of his life, as he is forced to memorise alphabets and nursery rhymes to give him a competitive edge over the other children. And if, God forbids, he fails to do accordingly, his parents take it as a personal insult, believing that the sky is about to fall upon them! Such extreme reactions and expectations are completely uncalled for, and form a breeding ground for the future shortcomings of the child.

Parents! Have you ever noticed how a child can easily memorise and reproduce any film or cartoon song without making a single mistake? Not only that, when you cannot reproduce it correctly, his reaction is to point out your mistake and go ahead and correct it himself. Have you ever wondered why this happens? The reason is as simple as it gets: he faces absolutely no compulsion in memorizing the song, and does so only because he enjoys doing so.

Learning is a natural process and most often a child learns through hearing and observation (audio-visual process). Man is curious by nature, children even more so. When a child enters a new, fascinating world, his interactions with the different aspects of this new planet start taking place, and his reactions to them shape his personality and his perspective. He crawls, laughs, takes his first step, starts talking during his initial development course. During these changes, parents can only support and encourage him. But they cannot and should not force him to grow according to their own wishes. A child should be left to grow, learn and mature at his own pace without the burden of expectations.

Every child is different, and in being so uniquely special, to start judging them according to a common yardstick is a big mistake. Especially when it comes to education, parents feel that it is their prerogative to ensure that the child behaves and learns purely according to their wishes, and leave the child without any options to explore his own choices and interests. Unfortunately, too many parents forget that their child, even though created in the image of themselves, is nevertheless, a completely different entity, and no matter how hard they try, they will never be able to inculcate the same likes and dislikes in their children as well. In fact, trying to do so only results in repressed ambitions, hidden anger and crushed self-esteem, which have devastating impacts on the child later in life.

Class or grade competition leads to jealousy, rivalry, aggression and revenge

It is not the ultimate certificate of your child's career or achievements

So for parents whose happiness revolves around their child's grade, a good grade is just a temporary relief from their child's achievements.

Seeing their child study by burning the midnight oil makes them satisfied.

Because whenever a child studies it needs some time to get stored in the memory circuit which is finely woven in one's brain. A child under pressure takes study as a ritual and tries to finish his curriculum as swiftly as he can. It may help fetching some good class-grade which is far from learning or comprehending... Hence it ends in a short term memory.

The expression 'short term memory' itself suggests that it stays for a short time, or soon vanishes. It occurs when one is nervous, restless and tries to complete one's syllabus fast; eventually it does not get encoded in the student's memory circuit and a child feels difficulty in recalling such learnt items during the most demanding time, such as at the time of his examinations..

Long term memory occurs when one studies in a comfortable way with the intention of comprehending the subjects meaningfully. So the study without any stress or compulsion easily gets encoded in the child's memory circuit which helps him in recalling easily. Moreover, it stays for a longer time.

Many of the suicides related to academics take place due to the lack of proper guidance and information.

So if a child studies two–three hours (depending upon the age) per day and is attentive in the class room teaching he can do wonders. Blaming academic pressure does not solve the problems. Parents should be smart and intelligent enough to understand the right methods of teaching as well as the process of storing of educational inputs.

Tips:

- Let your child enjoy his childhood. Believe in natural growth with healthy manure, sprinkle the required water and keep patience to have good fruits. The child finds his own vocation when he is given a chance to intermix with his age group. So it's always advisable to leave them in company, even to find a companion for the child if he feels too shy to socialize. These will add vital brownie points to your CV.
- Learn to change: change does not indicate your powerlessness, instead it indicates your friendliness.
- Exercise to keep yourself cool: remember your icons as role models whose sole responsibility is to influence their child with their own positive traits.
- Develop your selves as special parents: keep your mind free from negative thoughts especially about your spouse and child. Dismiss unnecessary arguments and doubts.
- Give respect to your child: unless and until you give him honour how will he understand the true value of it?
- Value the instructions or suggestions of your child: This practical and helpful way of teaching has a long-lasting impact on them. That is why we say: **As you sow, so shall you reap.**

Parents! If you sacrifice some of your pleasures in the first part of your life for the benefit of your child you will certainly enjoy your later life with a clear conscience.

❑❑❑

ANNEXURE-1

Awareness regarding the welfare of children has brought about a revolution in the field of parenting. Now many parents, including the father, are looking for the right ways to make their child a good citizen and a happy child. They come prepared to show their efficiency or try to learn if they lack some major skill without any embarrassment. Some parents come without doing their home work. When they start narrating about the negative behaviour of their child they often ignore the importance of knowing how they react in such situations.

Parents! Why don't you adopt the following method to remember? BEGIN KEEPING A DIARY, A DIARY ON PARENTING!

Let us assume that the father is keeping a diary on his daughter.

Make a Diary with the title "My child: My asset" MAKE ENTrIES DAILY/WEEKLY/PErIODICALLY.

Child's behaviour: Write down all the instances of her undesirable behaviour.
Your reactions: [one or more of the following] Ignore, keep mum, verbal anger, hidden anger, corporal punishment, sensitive to her problems, give suggestions actively, give suggestions passively, pass on to your spouse by showing the instance of undesirable behaviour. Child's problem: How do you deal with it? [one or more of the following ways] Scold, blame, compare, make her more confused, pass on to your spouse, listen patiently and discuss, avoid, postpone for tomorrow.
Child's wishes (Outing, travelling and visiting amusement parks etc.) Reaction: [one or more of the following] Start yelling & making her a culprit for poor performance in class, deprive her of recreations, make excuses, avoid, show your financial limitations, promise but never keep it.
Child's school complaints:
Reaction: [one or more of the following] Beat, scold, stop talking and loving, stop giving her privileges, talk to her patiently, meet the teachers to know the genuine problems.

Child's grumbling over the food: Your counter-reactions: [one or more of the following] Go on nagging till she finishes her meal, scold, beat, do not pay much attention, watch her reactions if you leave her without pampering.
Child's mood regarding studies: Your counter-reactions [one or more of the following] Start preaching, scold, beat, shout, sit with her to help in studies forcibly, sit with her to help in studies amiably.

A doctor-parent goes through lots of patients' case histories, check up, investigations, studies the medical reports etc. Why cannot they keep a diary for their own child's development record, particuiarly the emotional and psychological aspects?

Similarly an actor, politician, engineer, officer, job-holder, businessman, and worker in any field (creative to corporate) have to keep all the documents of their work-related areas, so as not to lose their status at their workplace whereas their own flesh and blood (child) is perhaps being badly neglected by them. Why don't they keep a record of their child's behavioural development so that they can work out solutions accordingly?

Parents! It is very simple. You can do it without disturbing your official agenda.

Essential guidelines for PARENTS regarding academic performance:

[Parents all over the world are chiefly concerned with their child's academic performance!]

Let us assume that the child is a daughter.

Set a convenient time specifically to assess yourself.

- □ You scold your child because her results/preparations are not up to YOUR expectation.
- □ Her poor performance affects YOUR social dignity.
- □ The child of your relatives/neighbours/friends has better record of academic performance.
- □ You are worried that if she scores poorly she will be deprived of future career opportunities.

- ☐ You appreciate your child while she studies burning the midnight
- ☐ You appreciate your child while she studies burning the midnight oil but become upset by seeing her report card.

Make a list ***once in a week:***

- ☐ What do you want from your child?
- ☐ Why do you want to control almost every desire of hers?
- ☐ Why do you want to make her a book-worm?
- ☐ How much is she really paying attention to her studies?
- ☐ What sort of ambience are you providing her?
- ☐ Find out how much quality time you spend with your child.
- ☐ Your career is more important than spending time with your child.
- ☐ You have a notion that your grown-up child does not need much attention.
- ☐ Do you give more importance to her class-grade than working towards her future goal?
- ☐ Does she have any special talent/unusual habit that needs special encouragement/expert guidance, and are you prepared to take the requisite step?

Assess yourself in an unbiased way. The above list will provide you an overall impression about your shortcomings, if any, and enable you to correct your approach soon.

Note that every child has a different brain and capacity. Their Intelligence Quotient and Emotional Quotient may differ significantly from those of another child. So comparison on this ground may be a blunder.

Parents! If you sacrifice some of your pleasures in the first part of your life, for the benefit of your child, you will certainly enjoy your later life with grace.

❑❑❑

ANNEXURE-2

Emotional stability is the only dimension of your personality which gives you the certificate of intelligence. A person with high Intelligence Quotient (IQ) and lower Emotional Quotient (EQ) is unlikely to be successful in the long run, and conversely, a person with an average IQ with high EQ is often a winner, because high IQ shows one's capacity whereas high Emotional Quotient shows one's capability to face the challenges of life. So if you have the capacity but you are not able to cope with demanding situations it shows your inefficiency in dealing with them. In psychological terms, it is widely known as COGNITION, which refers to one's perception, way of thinking, remembering and recalling. In a nut shell, it shows your problem solving skill. Lack of problems solving skill is the root of all troubles, and woes. Thus, problems with cognition may lead to disorientation, depression, anxiety, obsession and many other kind of psychological disturbances making an individual confused and misguided.

How well do you get along with your child?

The following statements tell a great deal about your dealing with your child. The most important is that the statements are in the form of answers so you have to be honest with yourself while selecting your own assessments and not be biased, otherwise you will miss the opportunity to correct yourself. Moreover, some statements may contain a reference to the "mother," but the intention is not to make them strictly applicable only to mothers. So do not be gender-biased. The mother plays a crucial role in parenting which cannot be overlooked. Both parents are suggested to answer each question. This is based on "Yes" or "No" response. You have to put √ mark if you find yourself in accordance with the statements; if not, put X. Scoring high does not give you the solutions. Parents! Be careful and clear, and truthful.

The following statements are based on the parents' personality which indicates how they deal with their child. Although the statements are this author's own formulations, they do not indicate any established parameter or bias.

1. I feel fresh in the morning.
2. I enjoy preparing food for my child.

3. I experience new food off and on.
4. I tend to give surprise gifts to my child sometimes.
5. I do not want to spend much time on phone calls while my child is around me.
6. Visiting ice-cream parlour/recreational places with my child gives me enormous pleasure.
7. I dislike praising my child without any reason.
8. My child often helps me while I cook something.
9. Discussion about sex with my grown-up child is not a big issue for me.
10. I think it is the parents' duty to inculcate a sense of time management in the child.
11. A child should eat on her/his own as soon as possible.
12. Without training and practising of time management, it is hard to make the child sleep and get up punctually.
13. I take parenting as an "art" which should be compulsory in the everyday agenda.
14. Parents without the skill of parenting cannot be considered as "Right Parents".
15. Overlooking child's needs and desires is an inexcusable crime.
16. The psychological needs of a child are as important as her/his biological needs.
17. I believe in the "early to bed and early to rise" formula and I tend to practise it.
18. I get lots of fun while cleaning teeth and having food along with my child.
19. I tend to tell a tale while my child is having her/his meals on her/his own.
20. I find telling a good story while she/he is having food is useful because it motivates her/him to finish her/his meals.
21. Leaving the child to the care of my assistants may mar the emotional bonding between my child and me.
22. It is a good idea to make a child eat of her/his own volition. As a prelude, start an interesting long story (like the Mahabharata,

Ramayana, Bible or any epic), and this should be continued during the next meal.

23. I find it is the easiest way to teach a child by making a summary of the subjects.
24. A child likes a subject in its easiest and simplest form so I follow this method.
25. When you adopt the "study-table" culture, it makes study tedious.
26. Teaching geography is not a problem. Geography is all about the universe and natural resources. The easy way to learn the subject is through interesting and practical discussions.
27. I discovered a child learns geography quickly with the help of a map and talk about states, capitals and various resources.
28. Solving mathematical problems is not a big deal for my child.
29. Mathematics has four functional operations—addition, subtraction, multiplication and division; one has to be familiar with each of them to know the entire family well—I follow this concept and teach my child accordingly.
30. I follow the easiest way to teach Hindi/English grammar through casual talks with my child.
31. I discovered several concepts to teach my child.
32. My child enjoys a lot when I teach her/him.
33. When my child makes mistakes in studies, I tell her/him to solve the problems on her/his own.
34. You are doing injustice to your child when you do her/his homework if she/he fails to do so.
35. General knowledge (GK) course is fun; I use it as a game.
36. A monotonous way of study induces fear of study in a child.
37. I find it makes a child more stubborn and disobedient when we apply a rigid method of teaching.
38. It is good if you give your child space to decide about her/his interest related to the subjects.
39. A fixed time for study is a good culture to adopt.
40. I do not upset my child's study period most of the time.
41. I tend to sacrifice my pleasures for the sake of my child's study.
42. It is hard for me to leave her/him in the care of assistants/helpers.

43. My child is free to be mischievous except in study time.
44. I believe a child has every right to enjoy her/his life according to her/his age.
45. Sharing one's childhood experiences, either good or bad (with care), brings a child closer to her/his parents.
46. I believe that a mother does not need a qualification, in order to teach her child.
47. I find giving emotional support is several times better than being a qualified person.
48. A positive mother alone can set an example of being a good parent. Watching television is part of culture and tradition. My child knows its limitations.
49. A child becomes a computer/television addict in want of other healthy activities.
50. Mother's positive worries (health, nature of eating, managing magazines, extracurricular activities, clothes etc.) makes a child disciplined.
51. I dislike giving gifts to my child every now and then.
52. My child is my best friend.
53. Parenting is my choice. I accept all the challenges cheerfully and respectfully.
54. I believe the ignorance of parents causes bad parenting.
55. When you enter parenthood, you again become a child by relegating to the background, in order to deal with the child effectively.
56. I believe "hide and seek" is the best game which you start playing with your child in her/his initial years.
57. Hugging, kissing, patting, playing with the infant child etc., are the best forms of good parenting.
58. Being used as a 'donkey' for the ride of my small child gives me great pleasure.
59. Appropriate punishment shows your concern towards your child.
60. Physical punishment takes your child far from you.
61. My child finds me a "great mom".
62. Touch gives a feeling of being wanted and loving in a child.
63. I enjoy sacrificing my work for the sake of my child's needs and requirements.

64. I do not find it wrong if my grown-up child has friends of the opposite sex.
65. I treat all of my child's friends well without being suspicious.
66. I believe being suspicious may ruin your child's attitude.
67. I enjoy her/his experiences with her/his friends.
68. I do not get panicky when I find contraceptives in my teenaged child's bag.
69. I do not feel hesitation in talking on the matter of sex.
70. If my teenaged child has some sexual curiosity, I talk to him/her sensibly.
71. It is unwise to give the child wrong information about sex.
72. I believe giving a child wrong information regarding sex is a breach of trust between the parent and the child.
73. Showing respect to older and other people is an indirect teaching of compliance and modesty in a child.
74. Profane language is a no-no for good parenting.
75. I believe the best way to remove the greed of money in a child is to give some opportunity to deal with money (pay to grocery, transport fare, bills etc.)
76. Dealing with money inculcates a sense of self-confidence and trust in a child's mind.
77. I believe quarrels on the money issue may turn your child into a criminal.
78. The stealing habit is an indirect method of showing aggression towards authority.
79. A problem-solver parent is the best parent in the world.
80. The trial-and-error method sows the seeds of a problem-solving attitude in a child.
81. I strongly believe that a child faces more ambience-and peer-pressure than academic-pressure.
82. I believe that the grade is a certificate given by the school while knowledge is an attainment reflected in one's personality.
83. I believe that paying attention in classroom is half of the syllabus completed.
84. Extra classes are an unnecessary burden.

85. I believe that the school teacher is the best guide.
86. I believe that healthy and regular discussions between the teacher and the student make a child confident.
87. A school-culture helps develop the personality as a whole, while extra classes destroy the flowering of one's own creativity.
88. Scolding a child harshly or unfairly lowers her/his self-esteem.
89. A child's self-respect is more important than anything else.
90. I ignore my child's outbursts for the time being because it may be an outlet of her/his own frustrations.
91. To check your child's aggression it is advisable to engage her/him in an appropriate and meaningful direction.
92. Most of the undesirable behaviour in a child emerges due to neglect in parenting.
93. A separate bedroom and spending maximum time in that room may help your child in building a strong and stable personality.
94. I never leave my child alone with any person I do not know sufficiently well.
95. The household work is usually divided. Everybody has certain responsibilities.
96. I allot household duties to my child according to her/his age.
97. It is a good idea to make your child's bedroom lively.
98. Without expression of your feelings you cannot be a good parent.
99. My child often helps me while I do laundry.
100. I believe that the peer group plays a major role in the development of a child's personality. So I, too, become friendly with them.

Result Analysis

If your score falls in the 10-20 range — your parenting is below average. If your score falls in the 21-40 range — your parenting is average. If your score falls in the 41-60 range — your parenting is above average. If your score falls in the 61-80 range — your parenting is very good. If your score falls in the 81-100 range — you are a great parent, deserving commendation certificate from the appropriate designated authorities

❑❑❑

ANNEXURE-3

Case 1

A nine- year- old girl was sitting in front of me with a thick medical file. She was suffering from symptoms of stomach ache, vomiting and restlessness, but no illness was diagnosed, in spite of several pathological and other tests.

Individual counselling was required to obtain information from this child. It took twenty minutes for her to narrate her horrifying experiences, which ultimately led to the diagnosis of child abuse.

In such cases, the role of a mother is critical. During counselling, the mother was unable to come to terms with the reality and started suffering from anxiety attacks. The mother's counselling became the priority and the **Cognitive Behaviour Therapy** was done on her. After sufficient counselling and therapy, the mother was finally freed of her anxieties.

Repeated counselling of the child improved her acceptance of the trauma, and emphasis was placed on the fact that she was not responsible at all for the situation. After making considerable effort and offering patient counselling, the child recovered her confidence, and the smile returned to her face.

Case 2

A twelve-year-old boy had developed a tendency of telling lies and often used to steal money as well. His parents were very restless because they used to get frequent complaints from his school about his poor concentration and inattentiveness in class. During a comfortable ***individual counselling*** *session, the boy showed his bitterness towards his family. He revealed that even the slightest of his confessions produced a disproportionately harsh reaction from his parents. This is how he gradually developed this habit of lying. The child was sad because he was often refused pocket money by his parents, even though most of his friends received pocket money from their parents. He was also quite depressed that his parents did not have an iota of trust in him.*

Family counselling was done on the parents. They realized the deficiencies in their methods of parenting, which, in their mind, earlier, was completely correct. A child needs acceptance from his parents which is entirely based on trust and other positive feelings. The parents were very happy to find a stable parenting guideline and their readiness to follow the instructions saved their child's future. The need for money is also a vital one among children today. Parents need to learn to educate their children on how to handle money, as early as possible.

Case 3

A child used to cry whenever he was ready to leave for school. His parents were very worried about his reluctance to go to school. He usually kept silent and had no interest in any extracurricular activities either. To exacerbate the situation, his appetite and sleep were also poor.

In an **individual counselling** set-up, the boy revealed his biggest fears: that in his absence his mother might leave home for ever. Moreover, he was very upset and depressed about the constant fights he witnessed between his parents. This made him go into a shell and he refused to talk to either of his parents.

Parental counselling was also administered. Surprisingly, the parents were unable to comprehend the fact that the consequences of their fighting could take a toll on their child in such a drastic way. They revealed that a lot of problems did exist in their relationship. As a result, they started coming for marriage counselling. They were advised to start spending quality time with their child and also to resolve their marital issues patiently, one by one. After following this advice, they were amazed to see the happiness and enthusiasm in their child. Their child had started taking interest in several extracurricular activities and all signs of shyness were removed from his personality.

Case 4

The parents were very perturbed due to their six-year- old girl's inability to pay attention to, and concentrate on, anything even for five minutes. They applied several methods, such as praising her, encouraging her, and even went to the extreme of scolding and beating her, but nothing worked. As it were, both the carrot and stick methods failed.

A **Behaviour Modification Technique** was applied to alter her behaviour. In this technique a child has to unlearn the previous undesirable acquired behaviour, and is taught the new desirable behaviour. In such a therapy, a consistent reward- and- punishment technique is used. The reward was given if she showed even the slightest desirable behaviour and a small punishment was given if she did not follow the structured plan. The reward was in the form of gestures and expressions of love and encouragement, and giving her some small incentives in the form of a chocolate or an ice-cream. The punishment included simply depriving her from these incentives.

After six months of therapy, she had acquired the ability to sustain her attention for longer periods of time and was taking considerable interest in her studies.

Case 5

Joe was addicted to television and computer. His parents adopted several methods to stop him watching TV or playing at the computer, but in vain. These methods included yelling, slapping, and depriving him of the rewards, e.g., going out and reducing his pocket money. Even their soft persuasion could not stop him from his TV or computer addiction.

Joe shared his feelings with me. He discovered that his sources of entertainment are the television and computer. His parents have no time for outings. He was blaming his parents throughout the sessions: "Whenever they are at home they shout at each other. They even blame each other or me for any mistake. My dad does not want to listen to anybody. So watching television and playing games are my only entertainment. I want to avoid their arguments. So the gadgets are my best friends."

Parental counselling was administered. They could understand their child's needs and desires. They started attending the counselling sessions. After that a turning point came in their life. They started visiting amusement parks and different places with Joe once in a while. Joe also joined sports club. All these changes had a positive impact on their child. Gradually, his addiction to watching television and playing computer games became less. And his academic performance was better than before.

Case 6

Surya, a 20-year-old boy, accompanied by both his parents, was sitting before me. He had lost a huge amount of money in gambling and still his demand for money worried his parents. They were surprised to find their son had no remorse at all. However, analysis of the case revealed that his mother used to pamper him from the childhood. He used to get a huge amount of money without any accountability. The easy money lured his passion and he used to spend it on clubs, parties and friends recklessly. His father also kept him at zero pressure all through his school life. So without being put to any exertion in making or earning money he developed a sense of immaturity in dealing with money matters. With his carelessness and want of proper supervision and monitoring he could not mould himself into a proper direction. But matters came to a head when he lost a big chunk of money in gambling that shattered his parents' composure. Where had the parents gone wrong?

Father's statement: "I was earning so much then why will my child be deprived of it? What's the difference between rich and poor then?"

He could not comprehend that his wrong concept of liberty and richness could become a big curse for him.

Mother's statement: "It's very simple, we've money and we give him. All the rich parents provide their children an expensive car, mobile and other gadgets. So where are we wrong?"

It is clear that both his parents had a clear idea that they were rich and their child had a basic right to possess the most expensive items, ranging from car to mobile. But why was Surya such a spendthrift and without any guilt feeling? The answers lie here:

His parents never discussed about money matters with him. At the age of twenty he was not given any responsibility.

He had no notion about how to earn money.

He was totally lacking in supervision and monitoring, especially in money matters.

His parents should provide him some ideas on how to spend money in a practical way. His father should discuss with him about his business and give him an insight into his past as to how much he had struggled before he earned so much and still he was struggling to make more or maintain his position. If the boy continues spending money in an irrational way, he may meet with misfortune very soon. He will not be able to develop his father's business and once a business stops growing it is hard to generate a spurt or reverse its downward spiral.

Case 7

Nisha, a fifteen-year-old girl, had frequent attacks of stomach ache and vomiting tendencies which kept their family in constant stress because all the medical reports were absolutely normal. During the counselling session she burst into tears and narrated her embarrassment, fears and shame. She had developed a soft corner for a man who was of double her age. She used to date him. But her immature mind developed a guilt feeling because she was keeping this a secret from her mother with whom she had so long shared her common and general problems. She wanted to tell her mother but she lacked the courage to talk about it.

However, mother's counselling was done. She took this matter very seriously. She started talking with her daughter about the relationship in between discussions on hormonal change and shift in attraction. Moreover she kept her daughter's issue very secret. She never discussed it with Nisha's father and her siblings. When Nisha shared her inner feelings with her mother she got an immense satisfaction and all her problems vanished soon. Now she is working in a reputed technical college.

Case 8

Prahalad's mother was strict and authoritarian while rearing her only child. He was not allowed to mix with friends and relatives who were inferior to his parents' status. Being a son of rich and famous parents he had to sacrifice his common and general desires to be friendly with the common people and connect with friends from less privileged backgrounds, and this made his life miserable. He wanted to mix with the friends of his temperament but this was frequently objected to by his parents. They drew a strict line about where to go and with whom to maintain friendship. As a small child he obeyed his parents. But the problem started when he left his home for higher studies where he found himself free from all restrictions. As ill luck would have it, he started making friends with each and every student. He was not regular in his classes. He used to bunk classes and had fun every now and then. When his parents got the report from the school about their son's irregularities and neglect of studies, they contacted soon.

The problem was that Prahalad's parents had an erroneous notion that making their child a bookworm was the key to success. Prahalad revealed: "They used to keep me away from any family and social celebrations. They never thought of what is going on in my mind. Now I don't want to study at all. I've lost all interest in my studies."

Prahalad's case is a cautionary tale for those parents who think that being a bookworm or studying by burning the midnight oil is the best thing for their child, for it is, instead, an expression of the parent's own complexes, insecurities and anxieties. These kinds of parents mostly think about their own prestige, rather than thinking about the happiness of their child.

Family, and social interactions make a child more confident and mature. A child who goes through lots of happenings easily develops a problem-solving attitude. Happiness is for those who can solve problems in a positive direction. So the way to success lies in one's problem solving attitude.

Case 9

Rudra, a fifteen- year- old boy, came with his parents. His parents were going through a hard time because their teenaged son was very friendly with students who were engaged in smoking and occasional drinking. And stalking girls was one of their hobbies. His parents wanted him to get rid of his bad company. Rudra had developed an excessive inclination towards his peer group. He was adamant that he could leave his parents but not his peer group. The rigidity was so much in Rudra that his parents were at a loss. They wanted to know the cause and remedy of his problems. In this case, Rudra was in his teens so he needed an exclusive ***individual counselling****, and Parental Counselling was also essential. The counsellor's first duty was to give Rudra an insight into his problems and talk to him sensibly and encourage him to solve the problems related to his undesirable behaviour, and tell him about the repercussion of his poor behaviour.*

In parental counselling, a counsellor advises parents:

Take your child into confidence first,

Do not say "No" too promptly.

Make a good arrangement at home so that the child can feel comfortable.

Keep in touch with the parents of your child's friend. Mind, never complain about his peers.

Keep the phone number and address of your child's friends. Interact with their parents off and on.

Invite his friends on birthdays or any special occasions.

Arrange some picnic or outing for them and try to participate with them.

Discuss the problem of your child and try to find out the solution.

Mohit, thirteen years old, all of a sudden slipped out with his friends to watch a movie. His parents were seriously concerned about his behaviour.

Parents should try to know the root cause of their child's behaviour.

They should arrange some entertainment. Watching movies, having meal outside occasionally with their child and so on may have a positive impact on the child's psyche and for getting a family bonding.

However, parents should be aware of their child's friends.

(All the cases and the character's given in this book are real. Only their names have been changed),

❑❑❑

ANNEXURE-4

Caution:

A global warning is given by the International Classification of Diseases (ICD-10, 1992) and the Diagnostic and Statistical Manual of Mental disorder (DSM IV) to be alert if a child is suffering from Conduct problems. Unfortunately, our children are suffering from these diseases widely without any proper attention paid by the parents or the families. They slowly develop the syndromes and when it becomes unmanageable, their parents find themselves the most unfortunate parents on the Earth. But the parents should take the proper steps by reviewing the surroundings, their own issues, peer-pressures and the temperaments of their children and their own which may be instrumental in giving rise to the behavioural problems in children before cursing or blaming anybody.

Let us have a look at the behavioural patterns of a child which may be dangerous in his later life if proper care has not been taken timely.

The International Classification of Diseases (ICD. 1992) has classified conduct disorder into two sub-groups:

1. **Socialised Aggressive Behaviour:**
   - **i.** children having bad company,
   - **ii.** truancy from home and school,
   - **iii.** stealing,
   - **iv.** loyalty to delinquent friends,
   - **v.** lying and setting fires.

2. **Undersocialised Aggressive Behaviour:**
   - **i.** children having temper tantrums,
   - **ii.** fighting, assault,
   - **iii.** destructiveness,
   - **iv.** uncooperativeness and
   - **v.** disregard for social values (e.g., stealing, lying, robbery, vandalism, drinking and rape.

√ Children with undersocialised conduct disorder show difficulty in accepting authority, which leads to conflict with parents, with school and with the law.

Similarly DSM IV has prescribed the following criteria of children's behavioural disorder.

The Children Below the Age of 10 Years

Oppositional Defiant Disorder:

A pattern of negativistic, hostile, and defiant behaviour lasting at least 6 months, during which four or more of the following are present:

1. often loses temper
2. often argues with adults
3. often actively defies or refuses to comply with adults' request or rules
4. often deliberately annoys people
5. often blames others for his or her mistakes or misbehaviour
6. is often touchy or easily annoyed by others
7. is often angry and resentful
8. is often spiteful or vindictive

Diagnostic Criteria for Conduct Disorder (DSM-IV)

Age 9-13 years

A repetitive and persistent pattern of behaviour in which the basic rights of others or major age-appropriate or societal norms or rules are violated, as manifested by the presence of three or more of the following criteria in the past 12 months, with at least one criterion present in the past 6 months.

Aggression to People and Animals

1. often bullies, threatens, or intimidates others
2. often initiate physical fights
3. has used a weapon that can cause serious physical harms to others (e.g., bat, brick, bottle, knife, gun)
4. has been physically cruel to people
5. has been physically cruel to animal

6. has stolen while confronting a victim (e. g., mugging, purse snatching, extortion, armed robbery)
7. has forced someone into sexual activity

Destruction of Property

8. has deliberately engaged in fire-setting with the intention of causing serious damage
9. has deliberately destroyed other's property

Deceitfulness and Theft

10. has broken into someone's house, building or car
11. often lies to obtain goods or favours
12. has stolen items of non-trivial value without confronting a victim (e. g., shoplifting, but without breaking and entering; forgery)

Serious Violation of rules

13. often stays out at night, despite parental prohibition, beginning before age 13 years
14. has run away from home overnight at least twice.
15. often truants from school, beginning before age 13 years
    - **Conduct disorder has increased risk to develop antisocial personality disorder in adult life.**
    - **Several researchers found a subset of antisocial personality which showed the following**

- **Psychopathic personality traits:**
- **Absence of guilt, shallow emotions, lack of anxiety, manipulativeness, superficial charm, and absence of meaningful relationships that are essential characteristics of psychopathic personality reported by several psychologists, (Mc Cord and Mc Cord, 1964; Cleckley, 1976; Hare, 1991).**

The other set of behaviour of children is dysthymic disorder. According to DSM IV, children and adolescents mood can be irritable and duration must be one year.

The following symptoms (at least, two or more, during one year) are present, while depressed:

1. poor appetite or overeating;
2. insomnia or hypersomnia;
3. low energy or fatigue;
4. low self-esteem;
5. poor concentration or difficulty in making decision; and
6. feeling of hopelessness (despondency).

❑❑❑

ANNEXURE-5

PARENTING MODELS

The following parenting style provides a full description about desirable and non-desirable methods of parenting (Baumrind, 1968). Assess your parenting style with the following methods:

Authoritative Style

An authoritative parent is one who—

- encourages and directs the child's activities in a rational way;
- considers the pros and cons of each action taken by oneself and one's own behaviour and, furthermore, the latitude and freedom enjoyed by their children as well as the restrictions imposed on them;
- exercises proper control over that child through a workable monitoring and supervision system;
- follows the rule of, "Give and Take" whereby parent should understand their rights as parents but must also consider the legitimate interests and volition of their child;
- knows that the authoritative parents approve of the child's present qualities, but also set goals and standards for his/her future behaviour and actions;
- is aware that the authoritative parents are those who assign reason as well as exercise power to achieve their objectives;

The authoritative parents have good monitoring and supervising quality. They themselves practise patience, self-control, and high self-esteem first. Their opinions are not based on the interest of group. They evaluate the situations and work, accordingly, for the welfare of their child.

Thus the authoritative parents are found to be more in self-control, rational, pragmatic, competent and capable of motivating their child in a right direction. The authoritative style of parenting allows the child to properly interact with his parents and feel free to seek suggestions from them. This pattern of parenting provides a transparency in parent-child rapport.

A child under an authoritative style of parenting has often been instilled with a sense of strong self-confidence, self-control and good communication skill, in comparison to his/her counterpart placed outside the preview of the said authoritative system. The former has a realistic attitude in his approach and so sets a realistic goal and works systematically to achieve it.

Permissive Style:

- The permissive parents often adopt an inconsistent parenting style. They fall on the lowest part of the scale in controlling their child. Generally, they lack control in maintaining a family rule and their lower maturity level does not allow their child to establish a good communication rapport with them. The environment of permissive parents is usually disorganized and disturbed. To reiterate, they fail to provide a good supervision to their child. Their lower level of monitoring allows the child to misbehave.
- As a result, the child develops low self confidence and immaturity failure in establishing and achieving any pre-determined goals. He is confused and confounded with several issues in the absence of any right kind of guidance, monitoring and supervision by his parents.

Authoritarian Style:

- The authoritarian parents often adopt a power-oriented parenting. They often follow an absolute standard which is approved by the higher authority.
- They force the child to obey them at all times and if he fails to do so, they often adopt a harsh method, by being more punitive towards the child.
- They harbour a misconception that inculcating such behaviour leads to a good future for the child. They are erroneous in their belief that the child will learn to respect authority, respect for work, and respect the preservation of order and traditional structure.
- The authoritarian parents are chiefly power-oriented persons. To exercise power on the child is the primary style of their parenting. The parents who belong to this group are highly exacting in their demands and, at the same time, less receptive. Thus, they are very

indifferent to their child's needs and desires. They usually apply their own demands and force the child to obey orders unconditionally. This pattern of style is considered to be the lowest in positive parenting style.

A child who puts up with the authoritarian trait by the parents, generally lacks discipline and courtesy. He has poor impulse control and, as a result, he becomes aggressive, hostile, frustrated, disobedient, revengeful, vindictive and vulnerable to any kind of stress.

❑❑❑